LIFE, LOVE
& everything in between

LEARNING HOW TO NAVIGATE IT ALL TOGETHER

DAVE & ASHLEY
CALLEN

Copyright © 2020 by Dave and Ashley Callen

All rights reserved. No part of this publication may be reproduced, distributed, or transmitted in any form or by any means, including photocopying, recording, or other electronic or mechanical methods, without the prior written permission of the publisher, except in the case of brief quotations embodied in critical reviews and certain other noncommercial uses permitted by copyright law.

Distributed globally by Boss Media.
New York | Los Angeles | London | Sydney

Paperback ISBN: 978-1-63337-404-1
E-book ISBN: 978-1-63337-405-8
Library of Congress Control Number: 2020940978

Manufactured and printed in the United States of America

TABLE OF CONTENTS

	Preface	V
1	Before Me Became We	1
2	A Rapunzel Story	9
3	Down But Not Out	19
4	Getting Back Up	27
5	Building a Strong Foundation	33
6	Honoring Dave	43
7	The Hardest, Easiest Decision	61
8	Not the Best New Year's Eve	69
9	Elephant Circles	79
10	When Life Hands You Lemons	83

PREFACE

A quick internet search will reveal the divorce rate in America is between 40 and 50 percent. Depending on which website you visit, there are different breakdowns by state, occupation, ethnicity, and so forth. You'll often read shocking statistics of first responder divorce rates in social media threads and online articles. While the validity of those statistics is often questioned, we can all agree there is no shortage of divorce in the field of law enforcement, and really in our culture today. We've known a lot of people who've gotten divorced over the past decade. Some came as a real surprise, which just goes to show you never know what's going on behind the social media feed.

At the time we're writing this book, we live in Las Vegas. Nevada is always near the top of the list of states with high divorce rates. This is purely speculation, but we would imagine the culture of Las Vegas plays a big role in that statistic. They say what happens in Vegas stays in Vegas—but that's not always true. Reading these stats, it would appear the decks are stacked against us: married law enforcement officer living in Las Vegas. That may be our reality, but we are determined not to become a statistic. As you will soon read, life has dealt us a crazy hand. We've had challenges that could've easily led us down the path to divorce, but we made the decision to fight for our marriage. When life gets tough you have two choices: be pulled apart or pushed together.

Getting married was the easy part for us. We both had careers, were secure in who we were, and knew what we wanted. Although we are opposites in so many ways, we clicked. Some might say our love story happened quickly, but it's ours and it's perfectly us.

Life, Love & Everything in Between

We've always been the party hosts. Holidays, summer barbecues, birthdays: if there's a reason to host a party, we'll be hosting one! It just made sense for us to have a destination wedding. We wanted our big day to be a reason for our friends and family to have an amazing vacation. And that's exactly what it was . . . a Hawaiian vacation with one heck of a party we called our wedding.

Standing on that beach in Kauai we had no idea what the next decade would have in store for us. We never imagined the hand we'd be dealt. They say what doesn't kill you makes you stronger. Well, we're a true testament to that! What almost killed Dave and had the potential to wreak havoc on our marriage, became the foundation we've built our marriage on.

We've laughed, cried, and struggled our way through the situations that have become the words in the chapters to come. We didn't always (and still don't) have it all figured out. Marriage isn't easy, just like life isn't easy. Just when you think you're figuring it out: PLOT TWIST! When we committed to writing this book, we committed to sharing our story honestly and as transparently as we could with you. Our hope is this book will encourage you and your partner to allow life's journey to pull you together and not push you apart.

chapter one

BEFORE ME BECAME WE

Ashley

There are quite a few things that make me unique, but two facts about me typically get a similar response from people: I'm a former air traffic controller and grew up in Alaska. Back in my single days my friends and I would joke about how many times this scenario would play out through the evening:

It's girls' night and we're sitting at a table enjoying a glass of wine (OK, more like margaritas because we were young adults and hadn't graduated to wine as a drink of choice yet.) It wouldn't take long before a couple of guys would make their way over and start with the small talk. Whenever it came to my turn to answer the question "What do you do?" their response was interesting. It would either be a comment that would lead me to believe they had no idea what an air traffic controller was, or they'd say, "Have you seen the movie *Pushing Tin*?" Bless their hearts, they tried. If it came up in the conversation that I was from Alaska, then I was basically a unicorn because they'd never met anyone from Alaska, let alone an air traffic controller from Alaska. "What's it like to live there?" they'd always say. Some nights I'd make a joke about polar bears living in my backyard or riding a dog sled to school and we'd all laugh—well, us girls would laugh, anyway. There were a couple times when the guys weren't totally confident I was kidding. Let the record show that I was; in all reality, I had a fairly normal childhood.

My parents were both raised in Fairbanks, AK, and most of my extended family also lived there. My two younger sisters and I were raised in an area of Fairbanks my dad's family homesteaded. I literally grew up next door to my grandparents, aunts, uncles, and cousins. My family owned a sand and gravel company, so we all lived around one end of a pretty decent-sized man-made lake. My childhood memories include riding on heavy equipment with my dad, tubing on the lake with my cousins, and huge family dinners every holiday. Fairbanks winters are long, dark, and very cold, but that didn't stop my sisters and me from sledding on the hill my dad would make for us in the front yard or ice skating on the lake.

When I was twelve years old we moved to Spokane, WA so my mom could pursue her dream of becoming an attorney and attend Gonzaga Law School. My parents packed up the U-Haul, and we headed down the Alcan Highway. Those were the days before cell phones and iPads, so I can imagine how long of a drive that was with a twelve-year-old, ten-year-old, and nine-year-old in tow. Most of the time we rode with my mom in the Toyota 4Runner, but if you were the instigator of an argument (or Mom decided you were) you got sent to time out: riding in the U-Haul with Dad. Whenever we saw Mom pick up the transmitter for the CB radio they were using to communicate, we'd hold our breath. Which one of us would get kicked out of the car this time? That's probably one of the reasons I'm not a huge road trip fan to this day!

We spent three years in Spokane and then made the move back home to Alaska, although we didn't move back to Fairbanks.

Instead we moved to the big city: Anchorage, AK. I use the term "big city" loosely. Anchorage is small by most standards (approximately 300,000 residents) but it's considered a big city by Alaskan standards. The move back to Alaska was a lot harder on me than the move out had been. I was in ninth grade and loved my life in Spokane. I had a great group of friends and hated that we were moving. I'll be honest; I was a brat. I refused to pack up my room and I'm pretty sure I made the drive back up the Alcan Highway completely miserable for everyone. I'm sure karma will have a hay day with me once my girls become teenagers. Oh well, at least my mom might get a good laugh!

The older, wiser me realizes what important life lessons this chapter in my life taught me: it's never too late to follow your dreams and moving is only scary until you make your first friend.

I obviously survived starting tenth grade in a new high school, and I'd even go so far as to say I had a great high school experience. I wouldn't go back, but I had as normal of a high school experience as you can hope for: above average GPA, great group of friends, varsity sports, high school sweetheart . . . and the cops never had to bring me home. There was that one time I insisted the cops call my mom when they broke up our graduation party, but that's a story for another book.

The real story behind this book began when I was twenty years old. I had a dream I was going to marry a police officer. Before you get the wrong idea, I wasn't one of "those girls" who was attracted to the badge or the uniform. It was legit just a dream I had once, and for some reason I remember it. Let's call it foreshadowing, because I've never had a "psychic moment" in my life. At this time, I was still living in Anchorage and attending the University of Alaska working on my degree in psychology. I was also taking flight lessons and working towards my pilot's license.

Flying challenged me; well, not really the flying part, more the landing part. I remember being so frustrated one flight and yelling at the airplane. My instructor laughed and sarcastically said "Obviously it's the airplane's fault and has nothing to do with the pilot in command." He was an awesome instructor, patient, funny (when he wasn't making fun of my outbursts) and a good sport. He squished his six-foot-two frame into a tiny Cessna 152, which wasn't an easy task. The inside of a Cessna 152 is small, probably smaller than the front seat of your car.

One particular training flight, we were waiting our turn to take off and started talking about my plans for the future. I'd be graduating that spring and knew I'd need to continue on to graduate school if I was going to have my own therapy practice. There was only one problem: I was burnt out on school. I had taken nearly double credit hours every semester and worked full time. What can I say? I've always been an overachiever. I actually thrive in chaos, which drives Dave crazy! As we're writing this book, we own two businesses, have two little girls, and are planning a cross country move. But back to that pivotal conversation. My flight instructor suggested I look into air traffic control. He thought I was a natural on the radio and it'd be something I'd enjoy.

The next day I met with my guidance counselor to inquire about the air traffic control program. An hour into the meeting I was enrolled in the program and on my way to adding an associate degree in air traffic control to my psychology degree. I've always been a "fly by the seat of my pants" person. I don't put a lot of time into making decisions; if it feels like the right thing, I go for it. Dave and I are different that way; I'm an emotional decision-maker and he's a logical decision-maker. Balances out nicely, if you ask me!

I graduated with my associate degree in air traffic control in December 2006. Back then, the Federal Aviation Administration (FAA) had a direct-hire program for college graduates. I had chosen the Western Pacific Region (WA, OR, CA, NV, HI) as my first choice. On December 26, 2006, I was offered an air traffic controller position at North Las Vegas Airport in Las Vegas, NV. I accepted and began my journey to where I am today.

Dave

I was born into a law enforcement family. My mother was a dispatcher for a police department in Las Vegas and my father a deputy/pilot for a sheriff's department in California. My parents were divorced, so I spent the school year in Las Vegas and summers with my father on Catalina Island. As a kid, I was always fascinated with first responders. Anytime I saw a police car or fire truck I wanted to see them in action and was never shy about asking to climb inside. I grew up with a love for aviation and was eager to follow in my father's footsteps. I knew one day I would fly helicopters.

I graduated high school and immediately went into the Navy. I worked as a plane captain (basically a crew chief) for an A6 intruder squadron on the USS Abraham Lincoln. Working on the aircraft carrier wasn't what I would call glamourous, but it solidified my love for aviation. Being in the Navy was an incredible experience, I had the honor of serving with some amazing people that I still keep in touch with to this day. It also gave me an opportunity to travel, grow up, and, most importantly, learn what it means to sacrifice. It is difficult to explain how much our veterans do for our country, regardless of what branch they serve in or what their job entails. Being deployed on the other side of the world, doing a dangerous job (with the only contact from family being letters that showed up sporadically in the mail) made me appreciate what we have in this country and the people who provide it. During this time, I applied for a naval flight training program, but I didn't secure one of the highly sought after spots. Even though flying in the Navy wasn't in the cards for me, I had a plan B.

When I got out of the Navy, I worked on the ramp for Southwest Airlines while I applied for the Las Vegas Metropolitan Police Department (LVMPD). Not only did I love aviation, but I was passionate about police work as well. LVMPD had an air unit, so I knew I could have a career that involved both my passions.

In 2000 I became an officer with the Las Vegas Metropolitan Police Department and quickly realized I had found my calling. At my graduation from the academy, my dad was able to pin my badge on in front of my family. This was a special moment for both of us as the path within law enforcement was continued and the torch was passed from father to son. Las Vegas is a destination like no other, and working patrol never has a dull moment. People come to the city from all over the world, some leaving behind their morals before they arrive. For seven years I chased suspects, got in fights, arrested hardened criminals, and protected the innocent. I also found a family within law enforcement with bonds stronger than anything you could imagine.

Being a cop is a job unlike any other. It's difficult to explain to someone that has never experienced it. A close friend of mine that is currently a lieutenant with my agency describes us as "servant warriors"—a label that I find extremely accurate. The kind of people that are drawn to law enforcement are a unique breed. We all seem to have a fundamental desire to help people while bringing to justice those that would prey upon the innocent. While our careers are extremely stressful and demanding, they are also very rewarding, and I honestly couldn't see myself doing anything else.

In 2007 I became eligible to apply for the Air Support Unit. I spent two months preparing for the testing process, an hour-long oral interview involving a ton of questions on department policy and aviation knowledge. This interview had, and still has today, a reputation for being extremely challenging due to the sheer volume of material required to study. It is also highly competitive, with several candidates testing for typically one or two positions. Officers in the Air Support Unit rarely leave; most stay with the agency, flying until they retire. I battled my nerves during the interview and eventually walked out feeling like I did reasonably well, but unsure of exactly where I would place on the list of candidates. The next day I received one of the most memorable phone calls of my life. I had placed number one on the list and was told to prepare for an immediate transfer to replace a pilot that had unexpectedly decided to transfer to another unit. Before I knew it, I was assigned to the Air Support Unit as a pilot. My longtime dream began to come true.

Making it to the unit was just the first step—successfully completing the rigorous initial training program was next. After eighteen months I earned my wings, and that's where our story begins.

chapter two

A RAPUNZEL STORY

Ashley

I've always been a relationship kind of girl. It's partially due to my "go big or go home" mentality. If I'm going to put time and effort into something, I have to know it's worth it.

December 2007. There wasn't much going on at North Las Vegas Airport. It was raining and pretty slow in the air traffic world. A few of us were sitting in the control tower counting the minutes until it was time to go home when the phone interrupted the ticking of the clock. A couple of our local police department pilots were offering to include us in their evening coffee run. Who were we to say no to visitors with coffee?

One of those visitors happened to be Officer Dave Callen. I wouldn't say it was love at first sight. There weren't immediate fireworks or a lifesaving moment where I fell into Dave's arms like in the movies. Pilots regularly visited the tower, and I'd never been easily impressed by a uniform. He was nice and held my attention with our conversation. When the tower tour was finished, he left with my number. Before you think, well aren't you sly, Maverick, know this: I gave him my number to set up a fly along, not a date. So when I got the text a few days later inviting me to coffee, I politely ignored it.

I was twenty-three, a year into my career, and decided for the first time in a long time, I was going to be single and focus on me. I had spent the past five years in two different long-term relationships, working, and going to school full time. As you can imagine, that didn't leave much "me time." I'm fiercely independent and have always prided myself on being in a relationship not because I needed one, but because I wanted one. At this stage in my life I didn't want one. My friends and I would joke about what I affectionately referred to as my "man diet." I wasn't going to actively pursue dating. Honestly, the thought of dating in Vegas seemed overwhelming for this Alaskan girl. I had convinced myself that I'd only be open to dating if the "right" person walked into my life. But I had no idea how to recognize Mr. Right. Turns out I didn't recognize him. Not at first. He was disguised as a police officer.

After some thought, and encouragement from a friend, I decided to meet Dave for coffee. What could it hurt? Having friends on the other side of the radio was always fun and I was new to Vegas and looking for *friends*. We decided to meet at a Starbucks near the airport after my shift was over and before his shift began. See a theme here? Let's be honest, coffee is life in law enforcement and air traffic control.

Am I the only one who dreads first dates? Always the same conversation: the who, what, when, where of our lives weaved throughout awkward conversation. The one thing Dave did have going for him was he knew what an air traffic controller was and probably wouldn't be asking me if I'd seen *Pushing Tin*. The timing of our coffee date was perfect. I'd be getting off work and he'd be going to work. That would make the end of the date, and goodbye, less awkward.

The day of our coffee date, I was actually really excited. I didn't bring a change of clothes or freshen up my make-up in the bathroom before I left work. Normally I would have stressed the night before over what I was going to wear; what would be dressy enough for a first date but casual enough for a coffee shop? I decided he had already seen me after an eight-hour day at work, and honestly, changing in the bathroom wasn't something I really wanted to do. I didn't realize it then, but this was the start of something different.

There's something about the ambience of a coffee shop. The hustle and bustle of customers popping in for their afternoon pick-me-up, the laughter of friends catching up over their favorite espresso drinks, people wearing headphones typing away on their computers. A coffee shop really is a great place for a first date; it's the perfect atmosphere to have a conversation.

Walking into Starbucks at 3 p.m., it wasn't crowded at all. Dave beat me there (he'll probably be early to his own funeral). Even though he was dressed in "normal clothes," he looked like a cop. He has the haircut that screams cop or military, but he also has a certain presence to him. He has this way of commanding the room, but not in that arrogant, stone-faced way. His smile softens his face and you feel a sense of calmness and security in his presence.

Sugar-free vanilla latte: twelve years later, and his Starbucks order is still the same. I'm all over the place depending on my mood, which makes our coffee orders a great analogy for our personalities. As we sat down at the table, our conversation felt different. Sure, it was a lot of the typical first date stuff, but it felt so much more natural. Maybe it's because we'd talked hundreds of times over the radio, or maybe it was all the things we had in common. We sat in that Starbucks for three hours, and Dave was almost late for work. He'll still say I'm one of the few people he'd get to work on time for (on time is equivalent to late in Dave's world), because I'm worth it.

Getting in my car after that first date, I knew it had been different. I felt the connection between us. The fact that he is ten years older than me and had a seven-year-old son from him previous marriage didn't matter. I knew I'd go on a second date with him. Knowing what I know now, he felt the same way. January 2008 is when our love story began.

Have you ever made a decision based on emotion versus logic?

Almost every decision I make is based on emotion. When Dave and I had been officially dating for about six months, things were going really well. In the beginning I was worried about how our schedules would affect our relationship. We didn't have the same days off, he worked nights, and I worked rotating shift work. But it turned out we did a great job maximizing the time we had together. My fondest memory from those early months was the weekend he took me to Catalina Island. Before meeting Dave, I had never heard of it! Dave had spent many summers there visiting his dad. It was such a special place to him and it would become a special place to me too.

Dave planned the entire weekend on Catalina, which was a nice change for me, the type-A planner. I was excited to see this piece of his childhood and spend three uninterrupted days together. We'd never had more than twenty-four hours together. We flew into Long Beach and took a taxi to the harbor to catch the Catalina Flyer. We opted to ride in the open air seats on the upper deck of the catamaran. Boy, was it windy! Every selfie we took, all you see is my hair. As we pulled into the Catalina Harbor I couldn't believe we were only twenty-six miles off the coast of California. It felt like we were a world away.

We did all the things that weekend. We rented a golf cart and cruised right past every "no rental carts allowed" sign so Dave could give me the five-star tour of the island. I saw everything from the Wrigley mansion to the old stump Dave had played on as a kid outside his grandmother's house. We sat on the bench that was dedicated to his grandparents, ate breakfast at the famous (to us) Pancake Cottage, and had ice cream at Big Olaf's. We walked along the beach and had beachfront massages. It was the perfect weekend getaway. Seeing the island through his eyes was amazing. I fell in love with the island that weekend, as I was falling in love with Dave.

Moving to Vegas wasn't really my choice. I didn't know it back then, but it'd been God's plan. When I graduated from the air traffic control program I'd chosen a region I'd like to work in: the Western Pacific region, which included Hawaii, California, Nevada, and Arizona. That was as much control as I had over where I'd start my career. When I got the phone call that I'd be starting my air traffic control career in Las Vegas, it was exactly that, where I'd start. Not where I'd stay.

As soon as I had completed my initial training at the North Las Vegas Airport air traffic control tower, I had put in transfer requests to a few different places. My transfer to Memphis had been accepted, but my transfer date wasn't until the following summer. At the time I wasn't in a relationship and had no ties to Vegas. I was twenty-three and ready to see the country before I put down roots. Why Memphis? I liked country music and I'd never been to Tennessee, so why not?!? Oh, to be twenty-three and carefree again!

Now I had a decision to make. Dave's career wasn't mobile like mine was. He had twelve years until retirement, which meant he wasn't leaving Vegas any time soon. We had casually talked about my upcoming transfer to Memphis when we first started dating but never really had a serious conversation about it. As the summer approached I knew I needed to figure out what I was doing. Since a twelve-year long-distance relationship sounded like an awful idea, I followed my heart, took a leap of faith, and turned down Memphis. It turns out that was the right decision because my conversation with the manager at Memphis wasn't pleasant. He wasn't very nice about the situation, and years later I learned he was an awful manager to work for. I dodged a bullet there!

When I told Dave I was staying in Vegas, he wasn't really surprised. Even though we hadn't officially talked about it, he knew I wasn't going anywhere. We were emotionally invested at this point.

The one thing Dave did was give me his word that when he retired I could choose where we'd put down roots. Seemed like a fair compromise to me! At the time I'm writing this we're months away from his retirement and yes, he kept his word. Thank goodness he loves the area of Georgia we're moving to as much as I do!

I'm hard to surprise. I'm pretty good at reading people and know when something is up. In August 2008 Dave did something unheard of: not only did he surprise me, but he left me speechless.

The sun had begun to set on the North Las Vegas Airport. I was working as the controller in charge, which meant I was the supervisor in the tower. Typically, the controller in charge didn't work one of the air traffic positions; they oversaw the operation and had the ability to monitor all of the frequencies. When I returned from a break one of my co-workers suggested I work the frequency and they would remain in the controller in charge position. I should have known something was up! No one *likes* being the controller in charge. But who was I to pass up an opportunity to work airplanes (and helicopters)? It was always more fun to work than it was to watch people work. Dave called to depart their helipad just like he had done hundreds of times before. He started making all these requests to fly here and fly there, which was abnormal. He wasn't usually that high maintenance, and he knew I didn't get paid by the transmission. I chalked it up to a slow night in police work and him wanting to hear my voice. He requested to fly by the tower (which was *not* abnormal—remember that Maverick reference I made earlier?) This time was different.

It was dusk, so the sun shades had been pulled up. I was going to wave as Dave flew by but he didn't fly by, he came to a hover.

"Tower Metro 5 with one last request."

[Insert eye roll from me.]

"Baby, will you marry me?"

WHAT?!? Is this really happening? I didn't say anything. I was stunned. *I didn't hear that right, did I?* I looked over at my co-worker with a look of shock on my face. "Say YES!" she yelled.

"Yes!"

A few minutes later Dave landed at the base of the tower. I had gotten off position and gone downstairs to meet him. It was then I saw most of the air unit standing outside the fence taking pictures. He had planned this so well, and I had NO idea! As I approached the helicopter, still in shock and trying not to cry, he got down on one knee right there in the dirt and presented me with a gorgeous diamond ring. It was a modern-day Rapunzel proposal.

Sometimes you just have to jump and find your wings on the way down. It doesn't have to make sense to anyone; it only has to make sense to you. Nothing about our love story made sense to anyone at the time. It was too fast. "Don't give up your career progression for a man you've only been dating for six months." "You're only twenty-three." Everyone had an opinion. I didn't listen to any of them. It felt right. I knew this was God's plan for my life and looking back, it was.

Dave

Anyone that has lived in Vegas can tell you we don't get many days of what most people would consider bad weather. Sure, it's a million degrees in the summer, but we seldom see low clouds and rain. So when we had one of those rare days where it was raining and the weather was so bad it kept us from flying, I decided to bring a couple of our new officers up to the control tower for a tour. When Ashley met us and brought us to the top, I was impressed with how she carried herself. Not only was she attractive, she was very outgoing and had an air of confidence about her that I wasn't used to. When she mentioned that she had gone on a fly along in one of our patrol helicopters a while ago and wouldn't mind going again, I got her number. My plan was just to schedule another flight. I didn't leave with the intention of asking her out, I just figured I would maybe get to take her flying and that would be the end of it.

After a day or two had gone by, I started thinking about her again. She seemed different in so many ways, and I decided if nothing else, I wanted to get to know her. Again, I had no intention of playing the dating game so I thought, "Hey, ask her to meet you for coffee!" That's harmless and wouldn't come across as a date. I actually went back and forth with the decision until I finally went ahead and sent her a text. I figured, *What's the worst that can happen? She will either say yes, no, or ignore me.* When she didn't respond at first, I thought, a) she's definitely not interested and b) note to self, maybe asking someone you don't know out to coffee actually is creepy so let's not try that again.

But she finally did agree to meet for coffee. When we sat down at Starbucks, my first thought was that this had a good chance of being an uncomfortable conversation that ended up with me leaving and being early to work that day. After talking for about thirty minutes, though, we really hit it off and the time just flew by. On paper, you would have never thought we would have been a great match. I have no idea how, but we really connected. Looking back, I think I actually was late to work (Ashley would say I was on time but on time is late in my world). One thing I knew for certain: I couldn't wait to see her again.

Driving away from her house after that weekend in Catalina I knew I wanted to marry her. By society's standards it was too fast. We'd only been dating a few months and I hadn't even met her family yet. But I knew. And who cares what society thinks? The only people our lives have to make sense to are Ashley and me. I was pretty sure she felt the same way, but there was only one way to find out. I had to ask her the big question.

A RAPUNZEL STORY

I knew right away how I'd do it. Aviation brought us together, so it only made sense that I propose from the helicopter. Now the biggest challenges were setting it up without her knowing and deciding when I should do it. There was only one evening a week when we both worked at sunset, so it took work to get the timing just right.

Because we worked opposite schedules, it wasn't hard to find the time to shop for the ring or make all the necessary phone calls to pull off the big surprise. We had plans to go up to Alaska later that summer so I could meet her friends and family. She was either going to bring me home for the first time as her fiancé, or I'd have a credit on Alaska Airlines because she'd be running for the hills and our relationship would go back to a professional one. I had high hopes it'd be the first option.

The sun was beginning to set. It was time. One of my friends I worked with jumped in the helicopter with me. He was also one of the pilots who had trained me when I first transferred to the unit. I started up the helicopter, looked over at him, and said "Here goes nothing!" *Let's hope she doesn't embarrass me,* I thought, *because four of my coworkers are driving over to the fence outside the control tower to watch the whole thing go down. If she says no, I'll never hear the end of it.*

I didn't know how I'd work in a proposal over the radio. I had about fifteen minutes to spare once I took off until the sun went behind the mountains and lit up the sky in a beautiful backdrop of color. I heard her voice on the radio and was happy that my plan was going perfectly so far. I had called up to the tower while she was on break and told them the plan and asked that they make sure Ashley was working the frequency. I hadn't planned on being high maintenance with requests, it just worked out that way.

As the sun went down below the mountain I saw the sun shades come up. It was now or never. I requested to fly by the tower and saw her inside. As I came to a hover I asked her the biggest question of her life: "Hey, babe, will you marry me?" You all know what happens next because you just read about it and we're obviously married.

When we went to Alaska and shared the story of our engagement, most of her family had the same reaction: you're showing us all up! They were joking, of course, but they were right. I knocked that one out of the park! They all wanted to know how in the world I came up with the idea to propose with the helicopter?!? It just made sense. Our paths had crossed at just the right time thanks to that control tower. If the weather hadn't prevented me from flying that night, we may have never met. She may still just be that beautiful voice on the other end of the radio.

chapter three

DOWN BUT NOT OUT

Police Helicopter (call sign Metro 5): Las Vegas Tower, Metro 5 two miles south of North Las Vegas with ATIS information tango, requesting bravo on patrol.

[Metro 5 just departed the North Las Vegas airport and is requesting permission from air traffic control to enter their airspace and patrol the area. ATIS information tango lets the air traffic controller know the pilot has the current weather.]

Air traffic controller (ATC): Metro 5 radar contact, altitude indicates 2,500 feet,[1*] cleared into the bravo airspace on patrol.

[The air traffic controller is identifying Metro 5 on their radar scope and giving them clearance to enter the airspace.]

The next thirty minutes is business as usual—patrolling the streets of Las Vegas from the air—and then the usual quickly turns unusual.

Metro 5: Tower, Metro 5 is going down.

ATC: Metro 5 say again?

The helicopter disappears from the radar scope.

Have you ever been in a situation where time stood still?

I was the air traffic controller and Dave was the Pilot of Metro 5.

---

1 * Altitude is mean sea level. The law enforcement helicopters fly 500 feet above the ground.

Ashley

Thirty minutes. That's all I had left in my shift before my weekend began. Dave was working day shift so we'd been able to spend the evenings I was not working together. The past year had been a whirlwind. We planned a destination wedding, bought a house, and I transferred from the regional airport to the international airport (which meant six months of training). We'd been home from our wedding/honeymoon for about a month and we were finally settling into "normal" married life. Well, as normal as two shift workers with opposite days off could be.

I was sitting in the tower wondering when my relief was coming back from break so I could go home when I heard Dave's voice come over the frequency. We have one of those unique situations where I get to tell him what to do at home and at work. Ha!

It was a typical afternoon at McCarran International Airport: airplanes carrying hundreds of passengers to their next destination, helicopters shuttling people to and from the Grand Canyon giving them a bird's eye view of the Las Vegas Strip, and air traffic controllers keeping a watchful eye over all of it. From the air traffic control tower we had a 360-degree view overlooking the iconic Las Vegas Strip and majestic mountains that surround Las Vegas. I've seen some of the most breathtaking sunsets over Red Rock National Park from that tower. Most days are uneventful, but not that one. That was one of those days you pray never happens. "Tower Metro 5 is going down." I thought those words would haunt me forever.

I remember thinking, *Did I hear that right? No, I must have heard that wrong.* I looked up at the radar scope expecting to see the little target with the letters MT5. But it wasn't there; that's when my heart started to race. There was a tour helicopter in the vicinity, so I asked the pilot if he saw Dave's helicopter. He should've been able to see him. He should've been able to offer me some reassurance that everything was OK, but he didn't.

I'd seen pictures of helicopter crashes and now they were all flooding into my mind. I turned around to tell my supervisor I needed off position but all that came out of my mouth was some form of "Dave just crashed." The entire tower went silent; they were all in shock at what I had just said. I was still working an active air traffic frequency and trying to hold it together. There were airplanes to get safely on the ground with hundreds of passengers on them and I needed to keep working, despite the tears that began to flow. It only took a minute for my co-worker to make his way over to my position and take over the frequency, but it felt like so much longer.

We'd been married less than a year. I kept thinking God wouldn't make me a widow before we even had an opportunity to create a life together, would He? Just a month prior we were sitting on the beach planning our life together. We were going to start a family and now here I was, sitting in an office, waiting to hear if my husband was alive.

Working in a male-dominated industry has its plusses and minuses, as you can imagine. I was sitting in my manager's office, wiping the tear-streaked mascara from my face, when he walked in with the only female member of the management team. He had no idea what to say about the situation and was clearly uncomfortable. I can't say that I blame him. Let's be honest, most men aren't particularly good at dealing with their own emotions, let alone a crying employee who may have just lost her husband. I appreciated his effort in seeking out our female supervisor. Her husband was also a pilot, so I'm sure my situation hit close to home for her. She walked in, gave me a hug, and sat in the chair next to me. We sat in silence for what felt like hours when the office phone finally rang. It was someone from upstairs in the tower. Dave was on the phone.

Twenty minutes. That's how long it took to find out Dave was OK. It felt like months. Sitting in the office waiting for a status report felt like an out-of-body experience. *Where is he? Why hasn't anyone called?* Then I heard his voice. A wave of emotions hit me: relief, sadness, anger. Twenty minutes? Really? I wanted to hug him and punch him at the same time. All I could think about was getting to where he was. I had to see with my own eyes that he was really OK.

Dave

August 12. A warm summer day in Las Vegas, and the weather is perfect . . . well, aside from the temperature being 112 degrees, that is. I took off early that afternoon to fly patrol with one of our newer officers in training, who also happened to be named Dave. For some reason there was an abundance of Daves in my unit, a problem that resolved itself when each of us earned a nickname. My partner had a particularly youthful appearance about him that earned him the affectionate nickname "Baby Dave" from the senior pilots. Not exactly an awesome fighter pilot call sign like Viper, Maverick, or Iceman, but you get what you get. Little would I know, at the conclusion of this flight I would forever be known as "Voodoo Dave." As far as experience goes, I was one of the more junior officers in the unit, with only a humble 750 hours under my belt. Eager to fight crime and make a difference in our community, we launched from the North Las Vegas Airport and started our patrol.

On this particular flight we were busy, bouncing from call to call assisting the officers on the ground. Flying a police helicopter is in many ways no different than being in a patrol car on the streets, we are just doing things from 500 feet up. As far as I was concerned, you couldn't ask for a better job. It combined the two very best career fields I was deeply fascinated with as a child: police work and aviation.

Flying towards the Las Vegas airspace I switch radios to the McCarran Airport tower and heard my wife's very distinct voice on frequency. I requested permission to patrol in her area and cracked a smile when she responded in a professional manor with just a slight hint of spunk. It's always fun to hear her doing her thing at work, and she is an absolute rock star at it.

Cruising along on the west side of the valley, we had some time between calls to catch up on Baby Dave's training as a Tactical Flight Officer (TFO). Tactical Flight Officer is the modern, high-speed, super-cool name for the "observer" that talks to the officers on the ground and handles the police side of our mission. We were right in the middle of a conversation when it happened—the engine began rapidly losing power and for an instant, time stood still.

Now I would love to tell you I had nerves of steel and inside I was calm, but that wasn't the case. If I'm being completely honest, for an instant I felt panic and a sense of denial that this was happening at all. I have heard stories from fellow officers involved in critical incidents where they were in a fight for their lives, having a gun pulled on them or being involved in a shooting, and "fight or flight" kicked in. Each of these people described a similar account; a sense of things going into slow motion while their senses were boosted into overdrive. This combination left a strong, dramatic impression on them for years to come.

It's important to point out that single-engine helicopters are very different from airplanes if the engine fails. Helicopters have the ability to perform a maneuver called "autorotation" that allows a safe landing to be made. The problem is, they descend very quickly. From our altitude we would end up on the ground in about twelve seconds and the options for a place to land were limited. We spend a great deal of time training this maneuver and most pilots go their entire career without actually needing to perform one. Here I was about to perform this risky maneuver in the middle of Las Vegas.

As we began losing altitude I quickly began trying to find a place to land. I remember beginning a right turn to line up with a street, only to find there were power lines crossing in the exact place we would need to touch down. With the "aircraft engine out" warning horn blaring in my ears, I could vaguely hear Baby Dave telling our dispatcher something that made me feel sick to my stomach—he called out a "444." The code "444" means "officer needs help—emergency" and is only heard over the radio in extreme circumstances, typically if an officer has been shot. As time continued to slow I remembered

Ashley was still the air traffic controller I was talking to and I needed to tell her what was happening. Even though I was extremely overloaded with stress, in that moment I felt a need to reach out to her. I was able to quickly key the radio and say "tower Metro 5 we're going down." Not knowing if she even heard it, I made another aggressive ninety-degree right turn and lined up with the only street left to land on. I vividly remember seeing two things: a white car driving ahead of us that was thankfully travelling the same direction, and some large light poles with yellow flashing lights that extended into the intersection we were about to descend into. We cleared the poles and touched down in the middle of the street, sliding ninety-eight feet before coming to a stop. Baby Dave quickly jumped out (in my mind, almost before we stopped sliding) and began updating the dispatcher with our location, also telling her we were down in the road but OK.

I then noticed the engine was still actually running, although it was all the way down at idle. I sat there for a moment completely confused as warning lights flashed and the audible "engine out" warning tone blared a rapid *beep, beep, beep, beep*. An investigation by our mechanics later revealed that the engine governor, a part that automatically keeps the engine at a set power level, had failed. The governor reduced the power all the way down to idle. Just as a car won't move with the engine only idling, the helicopter definitely can't fly.

As expected, several patrol vehicles from my agency quickly swarmed into the area and shut down intersections. As I climbed out of the helicopter, I was still reeling from the adrenaline dump and trying to process what had just happened.

Before I knew it, I had quite a few people asking a lot of questions so that notifications could be made and the scene could be managed. A bit overwhelmed with the situation, I made the most epic husband fail ever—I didn't think to call Ashley right away. As she will tell you, this might have been even worse for her than hearing me tell her we were going down. She had no idea for what felt like an eternity that we were even alive.

Ashley

When we started dating, Dave told me if anything ever happened he'd send a police car to get me. There I stood outside of the tower holding my purse and lunchbox. I looked as if I was waiting on a bus, not a police car.

When my manager and I had left the tower, I'd stopped at the nineteenth floor to collect my belongings. I'm not sure why I felt the need to collect my things right then. Maybe I had been scared of receiving bad news and feared that if I didn't get them then, I might never come back to get them. I didn't say anything to anyone as I walked over to the refrigerator and pulled out my lunchbox. It was obvious I had been crying so I'm sure the couple of my co-workers sitting around the table wondered what was wrong. I quickly got back into the elevator, where my manager was holding the door waiting for me, without saying a word.

As the police car drove through the security gate towards where I was standing, I felt a sense of relief. It had only been about forty-five minutes since everything happened, but I felt like I'd been waiting to see Dave for hours. I wasn't sure what to expect as we headed to the scene of the non-crash. Dave doesn't like when I refer to this incident as a crash. He always says, "It wasn't a crash; it was an emergency landing." Well, it sure felt like a crash to me!

I slid into the front seat of the police car and thanked the officer for coming to pick me up. As we drove I sat there holding my purse and lunchbox listening to the patrol radio. The dispatchers and officers were talking in codes that I didn't understand. I wondered if this was what the air traffic frequencies sound like to those not in the aviation field—words and phrases that might as well be another language. The officer broke my train of thought when he told me everything was OK and Dave did a fantastic job. There were no injuries and there was no damage to the helicopter. He was so kind to me and must have known how scared I was. I'm sure Dave had told him I was the controller working when he requested a patrol unit to pick me up. As we approached the street he had landed on, I'd never been so happy to see flashing red and blue lights.

Dave met me at the car as we pulled up. He seemed so calm given what had just happened. He was more concerned with how I was doing and apologetic for not calling sooner. The past hour I'd had so many horrible visions of helicopter crashes going through my mind. I'd been mentally preparing myself to walk into a scene from a movie, so I was surprised to see the helicopter sitting perfectly in the middle of the street.

The media beat me to the scene, so Dave and I were ushered into the back of a department SUV to avoid being bombarded by the reporters. The last thing I wanted was for the story behind the story to get out. I can just see the headline now: "Air Traffic Controller Frantically Searches for Husband after Police Helicopter Goes Down in Las Vegas Neighborhood." Everything in air traffic is recorded, and I didn't want the news stations playing the audio on repeat. Luckily the recordings are only kept for forty-five days, so we're in the clear now!

Dave and I actually have the recording of the incident and play it when we speak at marriage conferences. When we began speaking I was hesitant to share such a personal, and vulnerable, moment. Standing on stage listening to yourself begin to cry isn't the most pleasant feeling, but that moment was real, raw, and full of emotion. We've always said if we're going to share our story, we're going to share all of it: the good, the bad, and the embarrassing (for me, anyway). We also have the recording from when he proposed to me. That's a much more enjoyable audio clip!

chapter four

GETTING BACK UP

Dave

A friend once told me, "The only time you can be brave is when you are scared." This statement is spot on. Whether you are afraid of heights, the dentist, needles, dogs, or sitting on a toilet in a seedy truck stop bathroom, the truth is the same. The only opportunity to display bravery is when you are put in these situations and decide to face them.

Now it goes without saying that sometimes we have a choice and other times we are thrust into a situation without warning. You can choose not to get on an airplane if you are terrified of flying, but you can't control when you get robbed at gunpoint using an ATM. In my case, I didn't wake up the day we landed in the street looking for an opportunity to improve my skills to cope with fear. As it turns out, fate had other plans. I didn't have a say in the matter.

Fear is an interesting concept. When you think about it, this emotion is designed to benefit us. Fear is a simple reaction that protects and keeps us from harm. Our minds are built to recognize anything that will potentially do us harm and respond accordingly with this sensation. Millions of years ago this concept was necessary to keep humans alive and needed to be based on instinct rather than knowledge. Move the timeline forward to present day, and the problem now is that in most cases, we are smart enough to know danger when we see it. Maybe a caveman didn't have the common sense back in the day to realize putting his hand in the mouth of a saber tooth tiger wasn't a great idea, but today things are different. Well, for most people, anyway. My point? Our intellect has evolved, but our instincts are still protecting the cavemen.

Let me give you an example. You might find this hard to believe, but I am actually terrified of heights. Like, bad. It's actually embarrassing how much it makes me uncomfortable. People always ask how it's possible for me to fly helicopters, especially in the realm of search and rescue, but somehow, I'm good with it. I can land up on the top of a tiny peak in the mountains; just don't ask me to get out and walk around! I attribute this to a control thing. Since I am the one in control of the aircraft, it doesn't seem to bother me much. Now the flip side to this would be if you took me up high on the side of a building and asked me to stand on a ledge. Even if I was put in a safety harness and tied to something solid with no way of falling, I would be in a panic. Even though logically I know I won't fall, my basic fear instinct kicks in and goes into overdrive. It's such a powerful thing—I can't just ignore it.

When our engine decided to stop contributing to the flight that day I went from being relaxed one second to being overwhelmed the next. As I said before, I would be lying if I told you I had nerves of steel and just did what I was trained to do. The event itself was very stressful when it happened. But it was over in less than fifteen seconds. The most intense part for me was looking for a place to land. After I got over the initial shock of what was happening, I was focused on finding a place for us to get on the ground. We had lined up with a street, but we realized there were wires where we needed to land and then turned for the only other street left. After dodging light poles and eventually coming to a stop in the road, it was over very quickly even though it seemed like much longer for me.

GETTING BACK UP

That night it began to set in. I didn't say anything to Ashley, my friends, or my co-workers. The thought of getting back in the helicopter and flying patrol again made me feel sick. Just ten minutes before we made our emergency landing we had been working a call directly over the Las Vegas strip. With all the congestion and people in the area, had we needed to make the landing the outcome could have been very different. I knew I didn't want to give up flying, but I was surprised at how much the incident was affecting me. That night after Ashley fell asleep I was lying in bed wide awake with just my thoughts, still trying to process it all. I did exactly what I was supposed to do, we didn't get hurt, and nothing was damaged. This situation was exactly what we trained so hard for, and the outcome was as good as we could have wanted. So why was I struggling with it?

The culture at the time in law enforcement was much different than it is now. If an officer had issues after dealing with a critical incident, they frequently kept it to themselves. That's not to say their agency wouldn't support them; in most cases, they would. The problem was mostly with the officers. The culture was such that we are all supposed to be tough both physically and mentally. Saying you weren't ready to go back on patrol after being involved in an incident was considered a sign of weakness. It just didn't happen. I now found myself in a situation that in some ways was more stressful than the incident itself.

I also questioned whether it was just me. I tried to imagine how the other pilots in my unit would respond. The more I thought about it, the more I began to think it was just me. There had been a few other incidents in the history of our unit that involved a great deal of stress for the crew, and I had never heard anyone seem to make a big deal out of it. In hindsight, maybe those folks felt the same way I did. On the other hand, maybe they were just born with nerves of steel. Either way, it didn't make me feel any better about my situation.

I didn't want to say anything to Ashley, because I didn't want her to think I was weak. Looking back on it now, I know that was ridiculous. But at the time that's where my head was. I really didn't feel like talking to any friends either. The last thing I was going to do was mention it to anyone at work, so I did the worst possible thing: nothing. I went back to work as if nothing had happened. Let me be clear—I wasn't overwhelmed with fear, thinking I couldn't ever fly again. I just had not given myself an opportunity to process the event and really didn't understand what I was feeling was normal. Honestly, I would argue the only thing *not* normal would be going through some sort of traumatic event and not feeling anything at all. Either way, I was struggling with it and did not open up about it until years later.

Showing up to work the next day, my sergeant asked me how I was doing. I basically told him I was totally fine and tried to play it off as if the incident was no big deal. Walking out to the helicopter to go fly patrol, I thought, *What am I doing getting in this thing?* One of them had just tried to kill me. But I made a conscious decision in that moment that I wasn't going to let how I felt stop me. I had worked so hard to get where I was and absolutely loved my job. The biggest thing I did to help myself get over it wasn't just deciding to get back in. It was accepting that I wasn't going to change in a single day. I just decided to take it one flight at a time. Over the next several months I continued to fly and began to feel much more comfortable. Eventually I got over the feeling of anxiety that it might happen again someday and felt confidence return. Besides, what are the odds of anything like that happening again, right?

Initially I was torn between fear and the love of something that had been my childhood dream. As they say, time heals all. I was actually on the fence for quite some time when it came to writing about my experiences and how they affected me personally. For a brief moment I considered what people would think, and how I might be judged for being honest. After giving it some thought, I realized there are likely plenty of people out there who have gone through similar experiences and might benefit from hearing about mine—people that more than likely had the same outlook I did, many of them in law enforcement.

Once a good deal of time had passed and flying became comfortable again, things went back to normal for me—or close enough to normal, anyway. I wasn't stressed or anxious anymore, but it had just become more . . . serious. Not that I didn't have a serious outlook before the landing, but now it was as if a little bit of joy had been replaced with vigilance. I looked at it as if I had been tested and was fortunate enough to have persevered. Little did I know that a few years later I would be faced with a much more difficult test.

Ashley

"You're really OK with him still flying?" If I had a dollar for every time someone asked me that, we'd be living the high life on a yacht in the Mediterranean. My typical answer was, "Of course I am. It's his passion. Who am I to stand in the way of what he loves to do?" That response was mostly true.

We were still newlyweds in the "honeymoon" season of our marriage when I was smacked right in the face with the reality of Dave's job. When you marry a police officer you know in the back of your mind there is a risk associated with the nature of their profession. I honestly didn't think I had anything to worry about because Dave wasn't "on the street," he was in the air. The likelihood of him being injured on the job wasn't very high, or so I thought.

It's hard to put into words the array of emotions I felt the day I lost him from my radar scope. The best way I can describe them is fear turned into relief with a side of anger. Anger seems like a strange emotion given the situation, but I think fear was manifesting itself as anger. That was the first time I had to face the fact that Dave's profession was dangerous. Up until that moment, it had been easier for me not to think about it. But that was no longer an option. I had survived those moments when I wasn't sure if my husband was alive.

There were so many questions going through my mind that day. *How will I not worry every time he gets in the helicopter? How can*

I overcome the fear of the unknown and not allow it to paralyze me? Will my faith be able to conquer my fears? Will I be able to completely support his passion for this career he loves so much? I'm sure those fears and worries weren't as clearly communicated in my brain at the time as they are in this paragraph. I was all sorts of a hot mess that day, yet Dave was as cool, calm, and collected as always.

Timing has never been my strong suit. I'm more of an "If it's on my mind we need to talk about it right now" person. I've learned the art of timing when it comes to communication over the years, but I'm still a work in progress. If I knew then what I know now, I would have used the "Is now a good time to talk about my fears?" approach instead of hitting Dave with a loaded question after an extremely stressful day.

As we were getting ready for bed, I couldn't help but bring it up. I walked into the bedroom and asked Dave if he was still going to fly. I wear my emotions on my face (and in my tone of voice), so I'm not surprised that Dave became defensive with his response. He couldn't understand why I would even ask him that. Did I want him to give up his dream job because of an engine failure that resulted in a textbook auto-rotation? It wasn't that big of a deal. It happens. End of conversation. His attitude about the whole ordeal just fueled my anger. He may not have thought it was that big of a deal, but I did! At this point in the evening we were both exhausted and nothing was going to get resolved. I decided to let it go, which is not usually my style. Maybe it was the emotionally exhausting day, or maybe I knew better then to start a big argument when all I wanted to do was curl up in bed next to Dave and thank God he was still here.

As I drifted off to sleep, I began to think maybe I was overreacting. Maybe it wasn't as big of a deal as I thought. Maybe I shouldn't worry.

chapter five

BUILDING A STRONG FOUNDATION

We're writing a book about marriage, so our marriage must be perfect, right?

Before we get too far into our story we want to preface all of this by saying we didn't always, and still don't, have it all figured out. We've spent over a decade learning how to navigate married life and build a strong foundation for our family. Sharing the hard season in our marriage isn't easy; it would have been easier to leave this chapter out. But we believe in true transparency, and in order to share how far we've come, we have to share where we've been.

Ashley

A common piece of marriage advice I received was to always remain best friends because eventually the "honeymoon season" fades and that's when real life begins. Twenty-four-year-old me would roll my eyes because I didn't think our relationship would change at all. We already lived together, we had a strong relationship, and we had the same vision for our life together. I didn't see how a marriage certificate would change any of that. The piece I was missing was that it's not the act of marriage that changes the relationship; it's how we, as individuals, grow throughout the years.

Every life experience changes us a little. It's something we may not even be aware of. Every situation, good and bad, will shape us into the person we'll become. We have to make a constant effort to grow together. I often wonder why couples who have been married twenty plus years get divorced without an obvious reason like infidelity. You'll hear them say we just grew apart and we aren't in love anymore. That's the type of marriage advice I'd like to offer: grow as individuals, but also grow as a couple.

Who we are as a couple in ten years won't be who we are as a couple today. That's OK! You probably aren't the same person you were ten years ago either. Hopefully you're a better version of yourself. We should be striving every day to be a better version of ourselves than we were yesterday and have a stronger, more connected relationship with our partner tomorrow than we do today.

So what's the secret to a thriving marriage?

A strong foundation.

I love the song "The Bones" by Maren Morris. It's about a relationship having a strong foundation and the couple being able to survive whatever comes their way. My favorite line is "the wolves came and went and we're still standing." The nursery rhyme "The Three Little Pigs" taught us the importance of building a strong house. We all have wolves that come into our lives and try to blow our house down. Is your relationship built on a foundation of bricks or hay? Will the first wolf that comes along huff and puff and blow your house down?

Here's the thing about wolves: they're tricky. Sometimes we don't see them coming because they're disguised as a job loss, an injury, or an eighteen-month-old who never sleeps. We can't wait until we think a wolf is outside to reinforce our foundation. It might be too late.

Over the years, Dave and I have reinforced our foundation. You could even say we built a new, stronger one. We believe that in order for a marriage to thrive—not just survive—the foundation of the marriage must be built on mutual respect, solid communication, and committed intentional love.

Mutual Respect

One person's career, dreams, or goals are not more important than the other's. Yes, there will be seasons where one might require more time and sacrifice, but that doesn't mean the other person doesn't matter.

Two careers in public service revolving around 24/7 shift work, 365 days a year created some interesting challenges in our early years of marriage, especially when we had our daughters. Our oldest daughter didn't sleep through the night until she was eighteen months old. After my maternity leave ended I was able to work day shift and Dave worked graveyard. Not the best arrangement for our marriage, but it worked for childcare. Looking back, it's amazing we survived that year!

We were two sleep-deprived parents who argued about sleep. I worked all day and Dave worked all night. We were literally tag-teaming parenting. We had opposite days off and I resented him for sleeping. I would be up all night and exhausted by the time he came home from work. He would immediately go to sleep and (if I was lucky) an hour later I'd be up with our daughter. When he woke up I'd be so resentful that he got an uninterrupted period of sleep. He'd suggest I should take a nap before he left for work, but that didn't calm my irrational post-pregnancy hormonal anger. Instead of communicating my feelings and coming up with a solution together, I got angry every time he stated how important his sleep was for his job. In my mind I heard him saying his job (and sleep) were more important than mine, which (for the record) was not at all what he was saying.

To be fair, the early years of parenting are hard. Even the strongest marriages can be tested, so if that's the season you're in, hold on. It will get better. We're now years past this season and have strengthened this area of our marriage (and we get more sleep now).

We've both gone through seasons where we had to pick up the slack for each other to achieve personal and professional goals. We no longer have resentment towards each other, because we know a time is coming when the roles will be reversed.

We learned the hard way that all resentment does is cause cracks in our foundation. When I feel resentment creeping in, because I'm human and it does from time to time, I try to replace those thoughts with excitement and gratitude.

Solid Communication

A lot of marriage problems boil down to lack of communication. We all think we're great communicators, but are we? Going back to those arguments about sleep: in my mind I had decided Dave thought he deserved sleep more than I did, so I heard everything through that filter. When we talk about those tough early years of parenting, he still thinks I'm crazy when I recall my perceptions of his feelings. To be fair, post-pregnancy hormones and lack of sleep did make me a little crazy!

Communication is key to a successful marriage, but it's not always a skill that comes naturally. It's taken us ten years to really learn how to communicate and be good listeners. To be honest, communication has been a learned skill for me. Back in the day I would've told you I was an amazing communicator. I mean, I talked for a living! It turns out I was a great talker but a not-so-great listener.

It wasn't that I didn't want to listen. My brain just moves a million miles an hour and I'm already thinking of my response (rebuttal might be a more appropriate word) while Dave is talking. Having a conversation with yourself makes it really hard to actively listen and understand your partner's point of view. We both had careers where we had to be 100 percent right, and we're both type A personalities. Great for air traffic and police work, not so great for disagreements. Too often we would interrupt each other, which made us both feel disrespected and unheard.

"Team Callen" has become our tagline (or hashtag in the Instagram world we live in today) but it wasn't always that way. For years we weren't on the same team. When there was an issue, we found ourselves allowing the issue to sit in between us and cause conflict. What we really should have been doing was joining forces to find a solution to the problem.

We still have to remind each other from time to time that we're a team when conflict arises. It's easy to fall into old habits of me versus him, especially when I'm angry or stressed. We have to be intentional about conflict and remember it's *us* versus the problem. We have to remain united and leave room for compromise.

Committed, Intentional Love

We all said some form of "until death do us part" in our wedding vows. When I married Dave I took a vow of committed love, which to me means committing to loving him every day. Let's be honest, there are days when I don't like him BUT I still love him and choose him every day. Emotions happen because we're human, but it's easy to get complacent. We both need to practice intentional love, especially on the hard days.

#dateyourspouse has become a popular hashtag on Instagram. It seems like such a simple concept, and it's something most people want. We all have the best of intentions, but then life happens (crazy schedules, kids, budgets, etc.) and it's one of the first things to get pushed to the side. We're guilty of this. We didn't make date night a priority. It was easier to find an excuse than to put in the work to make it happen. The one or two nights a week we were both home, I had to work extremely early the next day; sitters are expensive, and I felt guilty for leaving the girls with a sitter when I didn't see them all day . . . and the list went on and on. What I was really saying every time I came up with a reason not to have a date night with Dave was that my marriage wasn't a priority. Reconnecting with my husband wasn't a priority. Those are hard words to type, but it's the truth.

What happened when we weren't practicing intentional love? We became roommates.

There was a period in our marriage when we acted more like roommates than husband and wife. We became complacent and got comfortable just going through the motions. We didn't see each other enough, we weren't intentional with the time we had, and our relationship suffered for it. Every phone conversation ended with whoever said bye first saying "love you" and the other person responding with "love you too, bye." Yes, that's how most married couples end a conversation, but we were on auto-pilot. Even though we did love each other, there wasn't intention behind the words. We just said them because we always had. They became just words.

The antidote to complacency is spontaneity. But let's be honest, the more responsibilities we take on, the harder spontaneity becomes. A last-minute date night out might not be possible when you have kids, but a spontaneous date night in totally is! Put the kids to bed and dance in your kitchen to your wedding song. Grab your favorite ice cream next time you're at the store. On a warm, clear night, pull down that blanket you got as a wedding gift from Aunt Sally, grab two spoons, and lay out in your back yard eating ice cream under the stars. Being spontaneous doesn't have to mean over-the-top. It's just the simple act of breaking up the normal routine.

Let's talk about something I think is unique to moms when it comes to not putting your marriage first: mom guilt. Man, did I struggle with that! Because I worked rotating shift work, I missed a lot of time with the girls. Only needing childcare a couple hours a week was important to Dave and me when we decided to have kids. That's why we worked opposite schedules with opposite days off. We knew we wanted to be the caretakers as much as possible, but we didn't realize the implications that would have on our marriage.

Valentine's Day 2011. Our oldest daughter was six months old. I had just gone back to work from maternity leave. No one was sleeping. We were emotionally and physically exhausted. Dave knew our marriage was struggling. He knew I was struggling. He planned a

BUILDING A STRONG FOUNDATION

Valentine's Day dinner at one of our favorite fancy restaurants and arranged one of our friends to babysit. It should have been a welcome night away for the two of us, but it didn't turn out that way.

I came home from work around 5 p.m., exhausted, but tried to be excited for our date night. I had one hour to get ready before we had to be out the door. As I sat there on the couch holding our daughter, mom guilt started to creep in. *One hour. That's all I'll spend with her today. By the time we get home from dinner she'll (hopefully) be asleep and since I work early tomorrow morning, it's Dave's night to wake up with her.* My irrational, post-pregnancy hormonal, sleep-deprived brain started to spiral. *I won't see her for twenty-four hours. I'm a bad mom. Yes, it's Valentine's Day but we're married . . . we don't have to go out to dinner.* Of course I didn't share any of these feelings with Dave, I just sat there stewing in my own thoughts. What had been a wonderful gesture from my husband, I'd now spun into "How dare he think it's OK for me not to see our daughter for twenty-four hours so we can go to dinner." I never said I was rational during this chapter of our lives; clearly I wasn't.

So, there I was, sitting on the couch secretly cursing my husband's name, when he did the unthinkable: reminded me we had to leave in fifteen minutes and asked if I was going to change my clothes.

In my irrational, angry state, I purposely took longer than fifteen minutes to get ready. Dave hates being late. I knew this, but didn't really care at that point. We headed to the restaurant and quickly realized how late we would be for our reservation. When Dave called the restaurant to let them know we were going to be late, they said they wouldn't be able to seat us because it's Valentine's Day and every couple in Vegas is out to dinner. He suggested we go somewhere else and then the flood gates opened. Every irrational thought that had been in my head came out. What was supposed to be a chance to reconnect turned into an argument. We walked in the door thirty minutes after we left.

Looking back on that time in our marriage, it's shocking we made it! We'll file that one under "for worse." The truth is it's possible to be present parents and make your marriage a priority at the same time. We know that now. Some of those hard times, like Valentine's Day 2011, could have been avoided if we communicated better, worked as a team instead of two individuals, and made our marriage a priority.

Our marriage is the foundation of our family and more importantly, our marriage is a model for our kids. It's taken a while, but I know date night away from the kids doesn't mean I'm a bad mom. It's quite the opposite. It means I'm a great mom who is committed to showing our kids what a healthy marriage looks like.

Dave

I'm one of those statistics. Ashley is my second marriage.

After my divorce I was jaded. I was new in law enforcement, a single dad, and had a lot of negative feelings I was carrying around as baggage. It's a natural reaction to automatically place blame on the other person for the relationship not working instead of taking a look at yourself. It's hard to admit to our faults and own our part when a relationship fails. That first marriage taught me a lot, and thankfully I met Ashley years later, when the dust had settled.

Going into our marriage I knew it wouldn't be easy. I knew we'd have our struggles and knew how much work it took to build a life together. I had experience; I'd been through divorce, custody battles, and all the hard stuff that comes with it. I'd had time to reflect on what went wrong and realized a lot about myself and how a relationship needed to work. I could have told you back then almost every issue comes back to communication skills, specifically listening skills.

If there's one thing Ashley and I have in common, it's our personalities. As you've read, we struggled with communication for years. I spent years communicating with the public patrolling the streets of Las Vegas, so you'd think I'd be good at it, right? It's one thing to interview a victim or a criminal, it's a whole different kind of communication style talking to your spouse, especially when she's angry and hot-headed. Sorry, babe, but I know you're all about being transparent and would agree with me. I don't want to throw her under the bus without going down with her. I sucked at communicating with her in the beginning. I interrupted her all the time, and that just made her angrier. I know now when I interrupt her it makes her feel disrespected and unheard, which was never my intention.

Learning how to parent together, when we were almost never together, wasn't easy. I had my parenting style and never had to think about what a spouse thought about it. My first wife and I had divorced when my son was an infant; I spent the first seven years of his life being a single parent. When our first daughter was born, it was a completely different experience than when my son was born. It was amazing to be able to share every moment with Ashley. We thought we were doing the right thing by working opposite schedules to minimize childcare, but we didn't realize what a toll it would take on our marriage.

We've learned a lot in the past decade. There have been proud moments and not so proud moments, but here we are. Sharing our story of struggles and successes with you. Talking about feelings isn't easy for me. As a law enforcement officer, and a man, I haven't grown up in a place where it's "normal" to talk so openly about your feelings—especially to complete strangers. I've seen so many of our friends' marriages fail over the years, and I can't help but think if this book reaches one couple and saves one marriage, it's all worth it.

The more we know, the better we are. We've been at this for over ten years now and we're still a work in progress. Every marriage is. We always have something to learn and can always improve ourselves and our marriage. That's the key to a thriving, not just surviving, marriage: never stop growing together.

If you are struggling in your relationship, or going through a tough season in life, it can (and will) get better. The fact that you're reading this right now is a sign you want a stronger, more intimate, thriving relationship. Either that or you heard about this couple with a crazy story and you're reading this for entertainment. That's cool too! Let's get on with it, shall we?

chapter six

HONORING DAVE

Dave

The first time I met Dave VanBuskirk (DVB) was the summer of 2004. We were both firearms instructors for our agency, which required us to help teach at least one academy class each year. Teaching the new recruits how to shoot was always a good time, and it gave us a week-long break from being in patrol driving a black and white (police car). DVB and I ended up in the same group and hit it off right away. We had a similar sense of humor that had us laughing at just about everything, including the recruit that almost shot himself in the foot. Hey, cops have a twisted sense of humor! But with all joking aside, I was really impressed with how well-spoken DVB was. He was a natural speaker and you could tell he genuinely cared about what he was teaching the new officers. He knew it could save their lives one day. I watched him go out of his way to make sure the recruits got things right. After that week we went back to our regular assignments and didn't cross paths again for a couple of years.

Life, Love & Everything in Between

  The year was 2006. I had been introduced to Brazilian jiu-jitsu by a good friend of mine and was absolutely hooked. It was around my second year of training in the sport, and I was finally getting to the point where I didn't get smashed by every single person in the gym. Living in Las Vegas gave me the opportunity to train under Sergio Penha, who is an absolute legend along with one of the most kind and genuine people I have ever met. Jiu-jitsu had become a big part of my life and was a great outlet to deal with the stress of being a police officer.

  One morning I was at Sergio's gym getting ready to train when who walks in the front door? Dave VanBuskirk. I had not seen him in the two years since we taught the academy class, but he greeted me with a huge smile as if we had been friends for years. DVB had a special way of making anyone he spoke with feel like they were a close friend. That was who he was, and it wasn't fake in any way; he was a great guy and very genuine. My first thought (we laughed about this years later when I told him) was "This guy is way too pretty to do jiu-jitsu. His face can't afford to get messed up."

  Over the next few months DVB and I trained at Sergio's gym several times each week and became good friends. We would spend a couple hours or so each morning on the mat, trying as hard as we could to submit each other along with the other folks in the gym. Often after leaving Sergio's we would go grab a coffee or boba drink around the corner, frequently getting suspicious looks when we walked in with bruises or a black eye. He wanted to test for our search and rescue section and I was studying to test for our Air Support Unit. We both worked hard that year and after testing we both ended up at the top of our transfer lists. Early in 2007 DVB was transferred to search and rescue, and one month to the day later I transferred to air support. As you can imagine, we were both ecstatic to make it.

HONORING DAVE

During the next several years we worked together while we learned our jobs. Both of us quickly discovered there was a very steep learning curve and it felt as if we were drinking through a fire hose. But over time we made it through the training programs. I was now a patrol pilot flying over Las Vegas every night doing my part to suppress evil and fight crime. DVB was working on becoming a paramedic on his own time, which would give him a much higher level of medical training than was required in search and rescue . . . but that was DVB. He was always pushing himself to the next level and he knew this would allow him to provide a much higher level of care to his patients. How hard he worked in every aspect of his life never ceased to amaze me.

As time went by, Ashley and I had our first child, in 2010. Our oldest daughter was born a daddy's girl and had me wrapped around her tiny little fingers. As you can imagine, things were tough with Ashley and me both working full time. She had a crazy rotating schedule as an air traffic controller, and I was working the graveyard shift. Between the schedules and having two kids—my ten-year-old son and a newborn—life forced us to shift priorities. I barely made it into Sergio's to train anymore, it was just too much to get down there. DVB knew I really missed it but he understood my family would always come first. One day at work, DVB said, "Hey, dude, come with me into the airplane hangar, I want to show you something." We had a smaller hangar attached to our main facility that housed our airplane, the SAR boat, dive gear, aircraft parts, and a gym that the rescue officers used to stay fit on duty. As I walked into the hangar I was shocked to see a large area of mats, framed in with custom wood to keep them in place next to the workout area. With a giant, sheepish grin, DVB said he had "acquired" them from the SWAT guys—who may or may not need them back at some point when they realize their extra mats were missing. He then spent two of his days off laying them out and framing them in so we could train at work together during our down time. I shook my head in disbelief, but it didn't surprise me one bit. He knew I really wanted to train jiu-jitsu but realistically wouldn't be able to for quite some time. He decided to take matters into his own hands to change the situation. Dave VanBuskirsk was just that type of guy.

In the summer of 2013, I was working day shift and had the same schedule as DVB. We saw each other every day and went on countless rescues together, with me operating as a co-pilot. I had been in the unit six years now and was nearing the point where I had enough experience, and flight hours, to be selected and trained as a rescue pilot. The rescue pilots all had a minimum of 2,000 helicopter flight hours. As flight instructors and the most experienced people in the unit, they were genuine badasses. My dream and long-term goal was to achieve this level of training and be able to fly rescues. Not for the title, but to be able to fly out there with teammates I loved and respected. The rescue mission in law enforcement is much different than any other aspect of policing. The people we saved were lost, stuck, or hurt to the point that we were the only ones that could help them, and that is an incredible feeling. The thought of being able to do that job with DVB and some of my other close friends in the unit was simply awesome. DVB and I talked about it often and joked about how crazy it would be for us to have that much responsibility.

On July 22, 2013 I was tired from flying patrol in the heat all day and went to bed a little earlier than usual. I woke up around midnight to the sound of my phone receiving a text message. Half asleep, I saw it was from one of my good childhood friends that I hadn't talked to in a long time. It said, "Hey man, I heard what happened and I just wanted to make sure you were ok." I was a little confused and figured he must have sent it to me by mistake, surely there wasn't a reason to say that. Not bothering to respond I then put my phone on silent, set it down, and went to sleep.

The next morning, I woke up earlier than normal. At around 4:45 a.m., Ashley was in our bathroom blow-drying her hair as she got ready for work. I rolled over and picked up my phone to find a ton of text messages and missed calls. The first message I saw was a group text to the members of Air Support from my sergeant. Still trying to wake up I could see that there was some sort of an incident during the night. As I scrolled through, I saw a message that would change our lives forever. "I'm sorry to send this out late but it was not initially confirmed. Dave VanBuskirk fell from the helicopter last night on a rescue and has died." I stared at those words and immediately felt shock and disbelief as tears began to well up in my eyes. Still holding the phone, I staggered over to Ashley, who didn't understand what was wrong with me. I tried to say something but for some reason couldn't; all I could do was hold out my phone and point to the text message.

Ashley said, "I will call into work and stay home with the girls, you need to get to the hangar." Driving in, I was in a state of shock. *How could one of our guys fall from the helicopter? Are they sure he's not alive? Is he missing? How could this happen?* When I got to work the sun had just come up and there were quite a few people there. The helicopter was sitting out on the ramp and crime scene tape had been put up on both sides of it to preserve any evidence of the accident. I stood outside for several minutes, trying unsuccessfully to hold it together and not cry. Eventually a pilot that I worked with every day came out and offered some kind words of support, and we went inside so I could find out what happened.

The guys had flown out that night to rescue a hiker that had gotten lost and eventually stuck on a ledge high in the mountains. This was something we did frequently. Upon locating the victim, the crew realized it was a tight area to get into and the rotor blades would be close to the terrain. These rescues are performed by lowering rescue officers and equipment down to the victim's location using a hoist. The hoist is essentially a winch in the helicopter that lowers and raises a cable with a hook attached to the bottom of it. This is all done while the helicopter hovers over or near the victim. To reduce the amount of time they would be so close to the mountain, DVB would be lowered down on the hoist and remain hooked up while he attached a rescue device called a "strop" to the victim. The strop was attached to the hook at the bottom of the cable and

DVB was attached to the hook as well. The plan was for DVB to stay hooked up to the cable and attach the strop to the victim, then both would be raised together.

At first, everything went as planned. DVB was lowered down and stayed attached to the hook. After a quick briefing he was able to secure the victim in the strop and they began coming up together as the cable was raised. A few seconds after they started coming up and the helicopter began to move away from the terrain, DVB became disconnected from the hook and the officer operating the hoist quickly announced to the crew that DVB had fallen. Initially not completely understanding what had happened, the pilot asked him to repeat what he said and the response was, "He fell! He's off the hook!" The pilot actually felt the shift in the center of gravity of the helicopter as this occurred and is one of many memories from that night everyone involved has struggled with.

After advising the dispatcher of what happened, the crew quickly began searching for DVB but the trees, bushes and terrain made it extremely difficult. Everything blended in together and as the minutes ticked by they struggled to identify where he might have landed. As the search carried on they also needed to offload the victim and get him on the ground to safety. After a time, the second rescuer on board stated what everyone did not want to admit: the distance DVB fell was not survivable. That officer was watching the hoist through night vision goggles, looking under the helicopter from the other side of the aircraft. He witnessed DVB fall and impact the terrain before losing sight of him. In a somber moment they all agreed and decided to land so they could transfer the victim to personnel on the ground. Once the victim was safely on the ground, they took off again and continued the search.

After several more minutes, the crew located DVB on a shelf of steep terrain and could tell he had not survived. As you can imagine, this was extremely difficult for the team members and they did an incredible job maintaining their composure while dealing with what is our worst-case scenario. As they attempted to maneuver the aircraft into position to lower a rescuer down, the weather began to deteriorate and the wind began to pick up due to small storms building in the area. With a second crew on the way to relieve them, the pilot in command made the difficult decision to land so the next crew could take over.

After a briefing by the initial rescue team, the second crew began to work their way into the area where DVB was located. As they neared, the wind began to decrease, eventually becoming completely calm as they positioned the helicopter overhead to lower two rescuers down. To this day I am convinced God intervened, calming the storms and allowing them to bring our brother home.

The investigation into his death later revealed there were no failures with DVB's equipment and he had done everything right. He became disconnected from the hook due to a phenomenon called "dynamic rollout," which we had not been aware of at the time. Without getting too technical, it is essentially something that can occur when using a hoist hook equipped with a non-locking gate. If the hook becomes unloaded, i.e., there is no weight being applied, any carabiners or attaching equipment can move freely and potentially into a position that will open the spring-loaded gate on the hook. The carabineer DVB used to attach his safety harness to the hook rotated up and over the gate and into a position that caused it to open a few seconds after his weight was applied to the cable. As soon as this happened the gate opened and he became disconnected, falling to his death.

The coming weeks brought anger, sadness, and questions that can never be answered. I felt so much shame that as I slept, my friend's body was being driven down the mountain with a large police escort. At the time, we lived very close to the highway leading to the area of the accident. As the procession of vehicles passed by, I was oblivious to the whole thing. I didn't know what had happened until the next morning. I wished I could have been there—that I had at least responded and done something to help. Not that it would have changed the outcome, but I felt an extreme amount of guilt knowing what those involved must have experienced.

I was raised in a Christian family and have always had a personal and private relationship with God. For a time, losing DVB brought me to a place that made me question my faith. But how do you continue to live in faith after your faith has been tested? DVB was the most genuine, thoughtful, and kind human being I had ever known. Why would God take him so soon? This was something I would struggle with for quite some time. It just didn't make sense, and it wasn't fair. It wasn't fair to his family, his friends, or the community he served.

I can now honestly say I don't believe we are meant to have the answers to such difficult questions. Sometimes you have to weather the storm, just like when you fly in bad weather. We all encounter situations that can make us question our faith, but imagine how our lives would look if we lost all hope and decided to give up. As they say, time heals all. I wouldn't say time has completely healed the wounds we all experienced after his loss, but I have come to be at peace with it. What changed my perspective over time was focusing on all the positive things DVB did with his life. Even more meaningful has been thinking about the impact his accident had on changing the safety of helicopter rescue operations across the world. As terrible as it was, the accident prompted the FAA to issue a safety alert informing operators of the dangers involved with the use of a non-locking hoist hook.

In the end, what carried us through was letting go and giving it to God—maintaining our faith in the journey life is and understanding there is a plan for each of us, even if we can't see it. DVB's actions that night saved a man's life. He will forever be remembered as a kind, compassionate, and joyful soul that was taken from us far too soon. There isn't a day that goes by where at some point I don't think about him. Even though he has been gone now for several years, those thoughts still bring a smile to my face. I feel extremely blessed to have had the honor to call him a friend, and even more so to work alongside him. He will forever live in our hearts and never be forgotten.

Ashley

I was up before dawn getting ready for work. The 4 a.m. wake-ups are the worst! The older I get the more of a morning person I become, but I'll never be that person who happily wakes up before the sun. That morning I had only snoozed my alarm once because I needed to wash my hair. By the time I was blow drying my hair I'd had a cup of coffee and felt (somewhat) human again. Out of the corner of my eye I saw Dave walk into the bathroom. I didn't pay much attention to him because I figured he was just using the restroom. As he got closer to me I could sense something was wrong. There was a look on his face I couldn't quite place. My heart skipped a beat when he handed me his phone. I had to read the string of text messages twice. I was in shock as I looked up and immediately recognized the look of panic, sadness, and disbelief in his eyes.

DVB's dead? How could he fall from the helicopter? Wasn't he attached to the hook? Are they sure? Have they found his body? Did the victim fall too? I couldn't wrap my head around what I was reading. I didn't even realize I was asking those questions out loud until I heard Dave begin to cry. "I don't know," he said. "I didn't hear my phone last night. I should have been there." My heart sank into my chest. I'd never seen him break down like this, and I could feel how much he was hurting.

I picked up my phone and scrolled my contacts for the tower number. It was still early and I knew a supervisor wouldn't be in yet. One of my co-workers, who was working the graveyard shift, answered the phone and, managing not to cry, I explained why I wouldn't be at work. I'd given up on drying my hair and quickly threw it up on top of my head in a messy bun. It probably looked amazing. Messy buns always look the best when you have nowhere to go. Am I right?

By the time I'd changed out of my robe and into a T-shirt and yoga pants, Dave was dressed and walking out the door. I quietly walked into each of our girls' rooms and saw them peacefully sleeping. I debated whether or not I should crawl back into bed, but as much as I would have loved a couple more hours of sleep, I knew I wouldn't be able to. I decided coffee was a much better idea and made my way down to the kitchen.

The sun was beginning to crest the horizon. It'd been about an hour since Dave woke up to the news one of his friends had died during a mountain rescue. Sitting in my quiet kitchen, with only the sound of my thoughts to keep me company, I began to think about DVB's wife. Did she know yet? Surely she did. I wonder if she was woken up by a phone call or a knock on the door. Her whole life had changed in an instant. Tears began to fall as I prayed for her. She was living my nightmare.

I can't imagine going to sleep and waking up to my world crashing down. We've lost officers over the years, but never one I personally knew. As much as losing a member of our blue family saddens me, this loss cut deep. This loss was personal because not only was Dave close to him, but his death was a result of an accident during a rescue operation.

Night mountain rescues aren't uncommon, and Dave frequently gets called out in the middle of the night for them. I couldn't help but think about the what ifs. What if Dave had been the pilot that night? What if the entire crew had lost their lives? What would I do in the situation where I had to tell two little girls their daddy wasn't coming home? Was I strong enough to be the mom they'd need me to be without their daddy? How do you grieve the loss of your husband while being strong for your children?

I needed some fresh air. I needed to get out of my head. I could sit there and "what if" myself all day, but that wasn't going to accomplish anything but make me crazy (and raise my blood pressure). The reality was my husband is still here—hurting emotionally, but physically OK. I walked out into our backyard and prayed that would never change.

HONORING DAVE

As the light of morning broke, so did the tragic news. I spent that morning fielding phone calls and text messages. Thankfully our girls were toddlers and didn't pay any attention to Mommy talking on the phone. All was right in their world as long as they had mini pancakes and *Mickey Mouse Clubhouse*. They weren't old enough to realize this was a Mommy work day and Daddy should be home with them.

Dave and I had worked opposite schedules our entire marriage to minimize the need for childcare. When we had our oldest daughter, we decided the sacrifice of not having days off together was worth having a parent home with her the majority of the time. After DVB's death, I started to question if our tag-team parenting was the best idea. Not just because I knew the girls would benefit from having both parents home with them more often, but because I missed my husband. We didn't spend as much one-on-one time together as we should have. God forbid something were to happen, I'd never want to live with that regret.

All morning I resisted the urge to call Dave and ask the million questions that were running through my mind. I could only imagine the stress their unit was experiencing. I knew I'd hear from him eventually and honestly, other than curing my curiosity, knowing all the details wouldn't have changed anything.

Knowing when to ask all the questions and knowing when to be silent doesn't come easy for me. It's honestly a struggle and something I have to constantly remind myself of when curiosity kicks in at the wrong time. The answers to all our questions will come in time, or they won't. We also have to be aware of why we want the answers. Are the questions coming from a place of fear and a need for peace, or are they coming strictly from us just being nosey? I'll be the first to admit I've been nosey a time or two (or ten).

It was late afternoon by the time Dave walked back through the door. The look of shock and disbelief had been replaced with sadness and exhaustion. The girls always got excited when Daddy walked through the door. He scooped them up and I knew he was hugging them extra tight.

Once the girls were in bed, we were finally able to have an uninterrupted conversation about what had happened. As I sat there on the couch with my legs flopped over Dave, I listened to the details from the accident. They sent shivers down my spine. It was a freak accident. He'd become disconnected from the hook and fallen to his death. I could picture everything as Dave shared the story. The pilot had known the moment DVB had become disconnected from the hook because he felt the shift in weight from below the helicopter. I can feel the panic in the hoist operator's body as he saw him falling through his night vision goggles, helpless in that moment. I can see the look of horror on the victim's face as he was brought into the helicopter by himself when just moments before DVB was on the hook with him. I can see the frantic search for DVB. I can feel the stress the pilot must have been under in the moment he knew they needed another crew because emotions and stress levels were becoming too much.

I heard the emotion in Dave's voice shift to guilt as he said "I should've heard my phone. I could have gone in and helped with recovering DVB's body." God always has our back and, in that moment, I believe with my whole heart, he had my Dave's back. As much as it pains Dave to admit it today, he wouldn't have been the best pilot for the job. Would he have done it? Absolutely. However, he knows he wouldn't have been his best self. How could he have been? He would have been flying into the mountains, in the middle of the night, in night vison goggles, to search for his friend who was possibly dead.

HONORING DAVE

We've been to a handful of law enforcement funerals, but DVB's was different. When we lose someone in our law enforcement family we all feel it, but this one was hard, really, really hard.

I can't describe what driving in that funeral procession felt like. As we made our way from the funeral home to the church, people lined the streets to show their support. Every overpass had a fire truck displaying an American flag and firemen saluting us on it. Driving down Las Vegas Boulevard, aka "The Strip," and seeing DVB's face on every major casino's sign was an experience I'll never forget. I'd never felt sorrow and honor like I did that day. I'd never been more proud of our city and the men and women who risk their lives every day keeping us safe.

I don't remember ever being as emotionally exhausted as I was the day of the funeral. I watched some of the strongest men I know cry. I held the hand of my husband as people offered their condolences. I hugged DVB's wife whose whole life had changed in the blink of an eye. I hadn't been able to find the words to say to her other than "I'm sorry."

How do you push through the pain and continue on when life doesn't make sense?

The weeks after DVB's funeral were filled with lingering questions. Dave found himself asking how something so awful could happen to as good of a person as DVB, but he never found any real answers. The truth is sometimes life doesn't make sense and we drive ourselves crazy wondering why and trying to understand. Sometimes bad things just happen. There's no other explanation than that. Knowing that and accepting it, however, are two very different processes.

Dave

You don't know what you don't know.

Dynamic rollout is the phenomenon that happened to DVB the

night he lost his life. Before the accident, our unit didn't know it was a possibility and didn't know a locking hook was available, or needed. We had never heard of dynamic rollout and were unaware there had been some previous fatal accidents. Sadly, this accident was preventable and stemmed from one simple issue—our own lack of knowledge within our industry. There was no negligence. Every person on the rescue acted exactly as they had been trained to. We simply didn't know.

We quickly learned there was a better piece of equipment available that would have prevented the accident—an auto-locking hoist hook. This hoist hook cost less than $1,000 and was what our helicopters should have been equipped with years ago. After taking a hard look at our operation internally, along with a safety audit that was conducted by an outside company, we realized another area we had been lacking in. It had been a long time since we had looked outside to keep up with industry standards of training and equipment. Had we been more active in this area, it is very possible we would have gotten the information we needed to have replaced our hooks. Our search and rescue officers might also have been trained to understand dynamic rollout and recognize how to avoid it.

As the years went by, I slowly made peace with DVB's loss. The cause of the accident, however, continued to haunt me and the thought that it was preventable shook me to my core. I felt very strongly that DVB's story needed to be told to the members of the helicopter rescue community to raise awareness and honor his memory.

Another one of my close friends, Jason Connell, felt the same way. Jason was even closer to DVB than I was—he had transferred to the Search and Rescue Unit in February of 2009 and spent the majority of his career working side by side with DVB. Cut from the same mold as DVB, Jason was in my platoon. We met on day one of the police academy. We became fast friends, spending the weekends studying and preparing for everything the academy staff threw at us.

We even ended up sitting next to each other throughout the entire process. I knew Jason shared the same dream to make it on the team, and both DVB and I were ecstatic when he transferred up to work with us.

The night of the accident, Jason was part of the second crew that relieved our team members who were performing the rescue when DVB fell. Jason was the first one lowered down and the first to be with him. He, along with his sergeant, recovered DVB and brought him home.

In 2017, due to a great deal of effort by Jason, we received permission from our agency to present the details of the accident at a large annual search and rescue summit. This event coincides with the largest helicopter conference in the United States and just happened to be in Las Vegas that year. In a large room full of our peers, many of whom had travelled in from out of the country, we detailed the accident. We also did our best to explain what an incredible friend and human being DVB was, in a venue so silent you could hear a pin drop. It gave us a small sense of closure to put it all out there and most importantly raise awareness for dynamic rollout. Quite a few people came up and thanked us after the presentation, offering their condolences and expressing how difficult it must have been for us to share. We were very thankful for all the support; however, the most impactful moment came just before we left the room. An officer from a rescue agency came up and showed us a picture of the hook they were using on their helicopter for hoist rescues. It was identical to what we were using at the time of the accident. Our message prompted that agency to replace their hook and might have prevented another accident.

One year later, Jason and I decided to take our message one step further and form a search and rescue training company with the goal of providing the best possible training to increase safety in our industry. We created SR3 Rescue Concepts—named after DVB's call sign of SR3—to honor our friend.

Ashley

I dealt with the loss in a different way than Dave did. I found myself drowning in fear. I have always been a heavy sleeper; Dave often jokes that I'm asleep before my head hits the pillow. It wasn't uncommon for me to sleep through the helicopter flying overhead or Dave's phone ringing at all hours of the night, but after the accident, I wasn't a heavy sleeper. Every time Dave was called out for a night helicopter rescue, his phone ringing woke me up and I would toss and turn until he sent me a text message letting me know he was back on the ground. For the first time in my life, I couldn't control my worry.

I never shared this worry with Dave. I knew he was still grieving the loss of his friend and thought about that night every time he got into that helicopter. I didn't want the stress of my worry to be the final weight that buckled him, and I didn't want to cause a wedge between us like after Dave's engine failure.

I had a choice to make. I could continue to live in fear, or I could live in faith. Dave wasn't going to stop flying (and he shouldn't) because of my fear of all the bad things that *could* happen. Dave's a phenomenal pilot. I wholeheartedly believe he is living out his calling. There have been more times than I can count when he has come back from a rescue and said the person would have died if he hadn't been able to rescue them. He's making a difference, and I decided my fears weren't going to stand in the way of that.

What does learning to live in faith look like, and how do you get there? It isn't an easy road, at least it wasn't for me. Once I recognized that my fear was paralyzing me, I had to figure out why. What was the root cause of this fear I couldn't shake? The inherent risk in Dave's profession wasn't new. I had been face to face with that reality years before, but it felt so much more real now. It had been easy to push my fears aside and not think about them, but now it was as if the flood gates had opened and they were rushing back in. I told myself over and over again to trust in Dave's training, trust in his abilities, trust in God's timing. As I prayed God's protection over Dave and the rest of the crew every time they went out on a rescue, faith slowly started to overpower the fear. I had a realization one night listening to Dave and some of our friends talk. They were talking about how if DVB had known that rescue would be his last, he still would've gone. The only thing he would've done differently was kiss his wife goodbye.

The fear of not being able to say goodbye: that was the root cause of my worry and fear. What if something happened and we were fighting? What if there were things left unsaid between us? What if I had to live with the regret that we weren't the best versions of ourselves with each other in the time God had given us? We could do better. We needed to do better.

Dave and I had been going through the motions of marriage for so long it was hard to change our routine. Admitting there is a problem and something needs to change is the first step. For me, though, making the change is the hard part. It takes work to not only make the change, but figure out how to make the change. I knew I wanted to have a deeper connection with him but I didn't know where to start.

I thought back to the early days of our relationship and how intentional we had been with our time together. We didn't have much of it, but we made the most out of every second we had together. We had gone from strangers to best friends and lovers in a short amount of time because our relationship mattered. How often do we give 100 percent to our relationship in the beginning and then years later find ourselves becoming complacent and giving 50 percent (on a good day)? I'll be honest, that's exactly where Dave and I found ourselves.

I had to recommit to my marriage. I had to become intentional and choose every day to put my marriage first. I had to stop saying "Love you too" out of habit and put thought and meaning into my words. I had to be the change I wanted to see in Dave.

Living a life deeply rooted in faith also means having a marriage deeply rooted in faith. It means having faith in each other and having faith that you'll get through the hard seasons together. Make a decision to have faith in your relationship and the person you married. Commit to having the hard conversations to better your communication. Prioritize date night and use it as a time to reconnect with each other. Make this your truth: we should never stop pursuing each other, or our relationship, just because we're married.

If something happened to your spouse tomorrow, would you be proud of the relationship you had? Or would you have regrets about arguments that went unsettled or date nights that never happened? Tomorrow is never promised, to anyone. If there is something on your heart, say it today.

A life lived for others is a life worth living. Dave's life will always be remembered as just that. Dave VanBuskirk died a hero. His memory lives on with all those who knew and loved him.

In memory of Dave VanBuskirk 1976-2013

chapter seven

THE HARDEST, EASIEST DECISION

Ashley

I was fourteen years old when my mother was diagnosed with an aggressive type of breast cancer at only thirty-nine. I remember her prosthetic breasts and how she would accidentally leave them on the coffee table. My mother is a fighter and one of the strongest women I know. She had something to live for and wasn't going to let cancer take that from her. She was determined to not only live, but live well. She came to every one of my softball games. Before she had her wigs, she would wrap her head in a scarf and sit there on the bleachers cheering me on. There's no doubt in my mind that my resilience, perseverance, and fighter spirit come from my mother. She beat breast cancer and recently celebrated twenty years in remission. Cheers to you, Mom!

Have you ever had to make a decision that seemed simple yet challenged you to your core?

Are you familiar with the BRCA1 gene mutation? What if I said the "Angelina Jolie" breast cancer gene? The BRCA1 gene mutation became a popular topic in 2013 when the actress announced she had undergone a preventative double mastectomy. I was already aware of the gene mutation because my mother had extensive genetic testing done. She is a carrier of the BRCA1 gene mutation.

My twenty-one-year-old self didn't want to know. I was already high risk for breast cancer and knew I had to be diligent with self-exams and mammograms. My breasts are part of my identity. I couldn't picture myself choosing to have them removed. I know that sounds vain, but that was my reality. I'm an August baby, so I was always the youngest in my class. That meant the last to get my driver's license and the last to develop (if you know what I mean). For years I waited for these breasts and the possibility I would have to have them removed wasn't something I could wrap my head around.

But then I had kids and everything changed.

I was 30 years old and sitting in a paper robe on an elevated table, with only my socks on, waiting for my doctor. My clothing was neatly folded on the chair, discreetly hiding my undergarments. Am I the only one who hides their undergarments from their OBGYN? I mean, let's be honest—we're about to get real close and personal, and I'm worried about her seeing my bra?

As I was sitting there trying to keep my palms from sweating so it wouldn't be super awkward when she shook my hand, I started looking around. The walls of her office were covered in posters and one caught my eye: "Are Your Genetics Putting You at Risk?"

Well played, God, well played. Yeah, they probably were. I had spent years trying not to think about it. I didn't want to face the fact that breast cancer was a real threat in my life. Eventually I would have to face the reality of the situation, but I had been successful at putting it out of mind, until now. My doctor walked in and broke me free from my thoughts. We chatted briefly about life and then she asked me the question, "Do you have any concerns or changes in health since the last time you were here?" For a split second I thought about saying no, but instead I mustered up some courage and finally talked to her about my family history with breast cancer.

It wasn't the actual conversation that scared me, it was what happened next. It was facing the reality of my situation and the potential decisions that came with it. Fear of the unknown has always been a cause of anxiety in my life. I've been known to overanalyze everything and worry about situations that have only occurred in my mind. I'm working on that. If I'm going to tell myself stories, I should at least make them have happy endings!

My doctor highly recommended I see one of the breast cancer specialty doctors in town. Whenever she says "I highly recommend," that's basically code for "You need to." So, naturally, I took her advice and made an appointment. *Here goes nothing.*

Walking into the cancer specialist's office, I was surprised at how full the waiting room was. Cancer affects so many more people than we realize. I looked around and there were so many women of all different age groups. I imagined some were young mothers like myself. Some had scarves wrapped around their heads and I knew they were in the middle of the biggest fight of their lives. I pictured my mother sitting in the bleachers at my high school softball games in a similar scarf. I couldn't help but wonder what their stories were.

My mother's genetic counselor had done a phenomenal job mapping out her test results. It simplified my genetic testing. A quick swab of my cheek, and we were done. I probably spent more time in the waiting room than I did in the examination room that day. Then we waited.

A couple weeks later Dave and I were back in that same office, sitting on that same elevated table, awaiting my fate. Deep down I already knew what the test results would be, but part of me prayed for the results to be negative—not so much for me, but for our girls. If I wasn't a gene mutation carrier, our girls would not be at risk of having that particular mutation.

Positive. It was confirmed. I had the BRCA1 gene mutation. The test results themselves didn't hit me like a ton of bricks. It was the question my doctor asked next: when do you want to have the Mastectomy? I wasn't sure. Did I even want to have the surgery? I knew I needed to and it should have been an easy decision. But my breasts were a part of me. They were a symbol of my femininity. As silly as it sounds to write, it was my truth. The part of the conversation I remember most vividly was the words "ticking time bomb." It wasn't so much a matter of if I would get cancer, but a matter of when. I remember sitting on that table giving my doctor every reason why the timing wasn't right. The biggest reason being the huge birthday party I was planning for my girls in the beginning of July (this was May). She suggested I have the surgery at the end of July. But my birthday is the beginning of August and then we roll into the holidays. The truth is I could have come up with a reason the timing wasn't right for every day of the year. She looked at Dave and asked, "What do you think?" He looked at me and said, "I think I don't want you to get cancer so you need to do the surgery."

End of July it was. Looking back I'm thankful they were both blunt and honest regarding the severity of the situation. The timing was as right as it ever would have been. I was consumed with the birthday party I was planning, which served as a nice distraction from what was to come.

I wasn't nervous until the morning of my surgery. I've never liked needles. I have those veins that are hard to hit and roll easily. Those in the medical field are probably cringing at how I described that, the same way Dave cringes at prime-time cop shows with crime scene investigators clearing houses. Every time I've had an IV it takes a couple different attempts and I end up with bruises on each arm. This time wasn't different. After a couple of different tries on each arm, my IV ended up in my hand. When the anesthesiologist came in to see me before surgery, he saw the IV in my hand and gave me a great tip. He told me I could ask for him to do the IV in the operating room for my next surgery. I'd be remembering that piece of advice for next time!

THE HARDEST, EASIEST DECISION

The surgery wasn't easy. What was supposed to be an overnight stay in the hospital turned into a three-day stay because my blood levels were low and I had a killer migraine. Turns out I had a reaction to the pain medicine, which was making me sick so I wasn't eating—which in turn contributed to my migraine. I was ready to go home. Luckily my doctor agreed and released me with the stipulation I would be in her office the next morning.

I looked, and felt, like death. Dave said I looked so pale I was grey. Thankfully he didn't say that at the time, because I was not in a healthy emotional place. I was a mess, emotionally and physically. I hadn't showered in days, wasn't eating, had a killer headache, and couldn't bring myself to look at my chest. And to top it all off I felt extremely guilty for feeling that way.

We were back in that same office and I was sitting on that same table. Only this time I wasn't in a paper robe. I was in one of Dave's oversized T-shirts that hid the four drains and pain pumps hanging from my chest. My doctor walked in, took one look at me, and told me I had two options: go home and eat a steak or go back to the hospital for a blood transfusion. Steak it was! She removed the pain pumps that were in my chest because they were contributing to my nausea. We decided I'd stick to Ibuprofen for the pain and forgo the heavier pain meds. We talked about how I was borderline to having a transfusion during the surgery and how I had chosen not to have one during my three-day post-op stay. Looking back on it, I should've had the transfusion. I was stubborn and stupid. Dave and I have that in common . . . you'll learn that in future chapters. I went home and ate the steak. I didn't want to, but I sucked it up and did it anyway.

I had four drains, two on each side, for two weeks. Dave was such a great nurse. He emptied them a couple times a day, gave me sponge baths, and washed my hair in the sink. We went ahead and filed those two weeks under the "for worse" part of our vows. I never wanted something so bad as I wanted to get those drains removed. Before my two-week checkup, I googled what level of drainage was acceptable for removal and made Dave promise to report that amount to the doctor. Luckily he never had to use that important piece of information because two weeks was long enough and the drains were removed.

The first few weeks following the surgery I fell into a low place. I questioned the decision I had made. I couldn't even look at my chest. Dave continuously reassured me it didn't look bad and once the reconstruction was complete I'd feel myself again. I appreciated his support but couldn't get out of my own head. I couldn't stop feeling sorry for myself when I couldn't pick up the girls or wash my own hair in the shower.

Even after I got the drains taken out and was able to shower normally and wear normal clothes again, I couldn't get myself to an emotionally healthy place. I needed help but my pride, and the quickness of the decision to have the surgery, got in my way. You won't hear me admit this a lot, but I was awful at accepting help, and even worse at asking for it. While I had the drains in, I didn't want any visitors. I really secluded myself. The only person I saw during those two weeks (besides my family) was my best friend, who the girls call Auntie Nikki. It happened so quickly I hadn't even told my core group of friends back home in Alaska that I was having the surgery. It wasn't something I put out there on social media, so very few people knew what was going on.

For the next couple months I went into my doctor's office weekly to have the spacers in my chest injected with saline. The spacers were expanding my chest cavity while I was healing and making room for the implants. One particular day the waiting room was really busy. There was only one seat available, and when I sat down I started chatting with the lady sitting next to me. She was my age. She had children the same age as my girls. She was such a beautiful soul, and you'd never have known she was wearing a wig.

We made small talk for a while and then she told me she was on her second round of chemo because the breast cancer had spread to her bones before they caught it. Right then and there I snapped out of it. I didn't have cancer. I wasn't sick. I wasn't fighting for my life and trying to raise my babies at the same time. God put her in my life for a reason. She was my reality check.

I left the office and called Dave. I burst into tears and told him I was thankful I had the option to take my health into my own hands. I never saw her again and I never had the opportunity to thank her for what she did for me that day. I still think about her and keep her in my prayers. I pray she beat cancer and is living an amazing life with her family.

About six months after the mastectomy I had the reconstructive surgery. This time I was ready when it came time for the IV. I asked the nurse if I could have the anesthesiologist do it in the operating room, and she happily obliged. While we were in the pre-op room waiting for my turn to be wheeled back into the operating room, another woman was brought into the room. Her husband followed behind, and Dave knew him! He was an officer in the same department Dave worked for. What a small world. She too had the BRCA1 cancer gene and was having her mastectomy after my surgery. I think seeing me on the other side of this huge decision gave her comfort in her own decision. I knew what she was feeling; I could see it on her face. I knew the struggles that would follow, emotionally and physically, but was able to comfort her and reassure her she was making the right decision. I shared the story of the lady in the waiting room with her and we both cried. I also gave her another sound piece of advice: if they suggest a blood transfusion . . . take it.

Being wheeled into the operating room completely awake was strange. I was surprised at how cold it was in there and how loud the music playing was. They gave me something to relax me through an oxygen mask and then I made myself look like an idiot. It was the same anesthesiologist as my prior surgery, who also happened to be good-looking. After he got the IV put in, he asked me, "How was that?" In my relaxed, drugged-up state, I said, "You're the best I've ever had." My doctor laughed and told him he better put me to sleep before I said something and really embarrassed myself. Thanks for looking out for me, doc!

Once I had the reconstruction, my chest looked normal from the outside. I filled out shirts, but I had scars. The first time I wore a bikini in public was on a cruise with some friends. I was really self-conscious about the scars. I worried people would see them and think I had a botched boob job. My friend basically shook me and said those scars make you a badass! You chose to make the hard decision to prevent getting cancer. That takes guts, and you should wear those scars proud like battle wounds! Once again, all I needed was to shift my perspective. And let's be honest, the only person close enough to see those scars is Dave, and he loves me for me.

As I'm writing this chapter, it's been almost five years since the surgeries. I hesitated how much I should open up about this. I want women to feel empowered to take control of their health, but I also don't want to scare anyone away from making the decision. The more I thought about it, the more I knew I had to be honest about the struggles. I want you to think, "If she can do it, I can do it."

I'm not braver than you. I have the same struggles. I also know we can do the hard things. Whenever I share this story I have women who tell me they couldn't do what I did. Yes, they could. This I know for a fact: we are stronger than we give ourselves credit for.

chapter eight

NOT THE BEST NEW YEAR'S EVE

Ashley

It's great to have family in town, but it's also great to get back into your normal routine, especially when you have young children. It was New Year's Eve and my parents had been in town from Alaska for Christmas. We said our goodbyes and they got into their rental car and headed for the airport. Goodbye always come with lots of tears (mostly from Grandma), but this was the first time my four-year-old got upset saying goodbye to Grandma and Grandpa. Luckily, distraction was still fairly easy at that age. Some milk and *Mickey Mouse Clubhouse*, and all was right in her world again.

It was approaching the best time of day for a mom with toddlers: nap time. Aka shower time for me! I was tucking the girls in for their naps when my phone rang. It was Dave. I silenced it with the plan to call him back once the girls were asleep. The phone rang again. I answered it with "Hey, babe, I'm putting the girls down. I'll call you back." All I heard was, "Paul and I crashed and I'm lying in the street" and then the phone disconnected.

Not sure if I had heard that correctly, I frantically called his phone back. It went straight to voicemail. Now I was in a full-blown panic running down the stairs with a four-year-old and two-year-old in a diaper in tow. I was crying and they were crying. I immediately called the hangar. There was a lot of chaos in the background. The pilot who answered the phone told me he didn't know what had happened other than they were injured and I needed to get to the hospital. I then did what every thirty-year-old does in a crisis . . . I called my mom. OK, maybe that's not what every thirty-year-old does, but that's my crisis mode. She didn't answer because she was going through TSA security. I called my best friend and before she even had a chance to say hello, I'm pretty sure I bombarded her with "Dave crashed and I need to go to the hospital" and then I hung up. I didn't plan on hanging up, but there was a number I didn't recognize calling. It was the officer in the ambulance with Dave. He told me Dave's back was hurt but he could move his legs and let me know which hospital they were headed to. I have to give Dave credit. He learned from the first time and made calling me his priority.

When we're in a stressful situation our minds go into fight or flight. Our neighbor was a SWAT officer and without thinking I called him and told him I needed to get to the hospital. He had just heard what happened and offered to drive me to the hospital. Thank goodness for awesome, level-headed neighbors! I turned around to see my two- and four-year-old little girls confused and crying. God had blessed me with amazing friends that had become family. The next thing I knew my best friend walked through my door, scooped up the girls, and told me to call her when I knew what happened. I'm not sure I said more than two words to her before I jumped into my neighbor's truck, but if there's anyone I would trust to walk in and take control of my house in any situation, it's her. There's a reason my girls call her Auntie Mickey (her name is Nikki but the girls have always called her Auntie Mickey). We all need an Auntie Nikki in our life.

I don't remember much of the ride to the hospital. It's a good thing I wasn't driving! My mother called me back and I filled her in on what was happening. She had Delta Airlines pull their bags off the plane, and they headed back to my house. As we pulled into the hospital I saw red and blue flashing lights everywhere. The officer who had answered the phone when I called the hangar was waiting for me as we pulled up to the front of the hospital. I jumped out and he ushered me in. It was a sight to see. There were people everywhere. We couldn't even get into the trauma department without someone trying to stop and talk to me. I just wanted to see Dave. The officer I was with did a fantastic job playing defense. Walking into the trauma department I saw a lot of familiar faces, including the wife of the officer who was with Dave in the helicopter. It was refreshing to see her; it almost provided a little calm amid the chaos. There was something comforting in knowing I wasn't in this by myself. I looked around and wondered where Dave was. I'm not sure if I asked that out loud or if the look on my face said it for me. One of the sweet nurses came over and let me know he was getting a CT scan and would be out shortly.

    I finally got to see Dave as they wheeled him into the trauma unit. In that moment I might have taken my first real breath since his phone call. I honestly didn't know what to expect. Would he be bloody? Would he be hooked up to all kinds of machines with IV bags hanging all around him? Surprisingly, he looked relatively normal, minus the neck brace. I looked around and realized this wing of the trauma unit was overflowing with doctors, nurses, police officers, and staff. All of a sudden I realized I hadn't showered. I might have brushed my hair earlier that morning. I had to double check to make sure I was wearing a bra. Thank goodness I was! Luckily I was in a sweatshirt, so you probably wouldn't have noticed if I wasn't. Go figure, the day I met the sheriff I hadn't showered, was in yoga pants and a sweatshirt, and my hair was barely brushed.

    I'm sure Dave will tell you in his part of this chapter, but he doesn't like pain medicine. He was lying there (still in his neck brace) in excruciating pain. I looked over to see his partner on cloud nine telling everyone he'd get in the helicopter with Dave right now. The nurse and I were trying to talk Dave into taking something for the pain, but man, he is stubborn! He started negotiating with the nurse asking for baby aspirin. [Insert eye roll.] I don't think that's going to help with the pain, babe! We finally talked him into taking a muscle relaxer and some Advil.

The doctor gave us some good news when he removed the neck brace so Dave could at least move his head. He had some pretty substantial injuries to his back, but he could go home that evening. Over the next few hours I made a lot of phone calls and we had a constant influx of people in and out of the trauma unit.

It'd been about eight hours since the crash. We were all physically and emotionally exhausted by the time we were released from the hospital. Dave was in a back brace and couldn't get up by himself. His sergeant at the time had been at the hospital with us and drove us home. He helped get Dave into the house but then he had to go into work. New Year's Eve is the busiest day for law enforcement in Las Vegas. Everyone works. That day it became a joke that the only way to get New Year's Eve off is to crash a helicopter.

After we got home, Dave finally agreed to take a pain pill. The closest twenty-four-hour pharmacy that was open on New Year's Eve was a twenty-minute drive from our house. You'd think there'd be more of them in our twenty-four-hour town! Once I got Dave settled, and medicated, I finally got to take that shower and wash away some of the day's stress.

Dave

New Year's Eve is an extremely busy day in Las Vegas. Every year more than 400,000 people come to the city to celebrate, the majority of them down on the iconic Las Vegas strip. Second in size only to the ball drop at Times Square in New York City, it's quite the party. As you can imagine, it requires a massive amount of preparation on the part of the Las Vegas Metropolitan Police Department.

NOT THE BEST NEW YEAR'S EVE

December 31, 2014 started like any other day for me at work. In Vegas if you are an officer and New Year's Eve falls on your day off, you put on a patrol uniform and work the strip that evening. Even the detectives and department members that work in plain clothes are assigned down there. The event requires that many officers for the safety of the public. Basically, everyone works on New Year's Eve. If you work the day shift and it's a regular work day, you work a twelve-hour shift in your current assignment. For me, it was a regular work day so I was covering patrol flights with some other officers in the unit.

The weather wasn't the greatest that morning. It was much colder than normal, and high winds were ripping through the Las Vegas Valley. Between the high winds and waiting for some maintenance to be completed on one of our patrol helicopters, we had not been able to fly since starting our shift. After lunch the winds began to die down and we were eager to get out and fly. Our mechanics had just finished completing an inspection that was required every hundred hours on Air 2, the helicopter we were planning on using for patrol.

Paul, one of our senior pilots and flight instructors, asked if I wanted to go fly. Paul had transferred to the unit the year before I did and was not only a great pilot and TFO, but a friend. Paul loved to catch criminals; he was one of the best TFO's in the history of the unit. When Paul asked me, "Do you want to fly or ride?" I told him I was good either way and he could decide. He replied "You fly, let's go catch some people." With that, we walked out to the helicopter and were quickly airborne. The time was 1:30 p.m.

Several years had passed since my landing in the street, and although always in the back of my mind, my initial anxiety about flying had greatly improved. As I said in the previous chapter, things had gotten more serious after that event, but over time I felt much better. I had also become a flight instructor and achieved my goal of becoming a rescue pilot. DVB would be proud! The training and experience I gained during that process did quite a bit to build confidence in my flying. Besides, statistically the chances of having one engine failure during a flying career in turbine aircraft are very low. There was actually a running joke with Ashley and the controllers in the tower about flying with me. We were authorized to take new tower controllers on familiarization flights while on patrol. Sometimes the controller would be nervous about flying. The other tower folks would always say, "Go fly with Dave, he's already had his engine emergency so you will be just fine."

As soon as we took off we received a call near downtown at an apartment complex. The details given stated a male was chasing a female outside with a knife. Paul gave me the address and as I turned towards it he quickly began gathering information as I tried to get us there as quickly as possible. Moments later we arrived overhead and I entered a wide orbit of the apartment complex so Paul could attempt to locate the building they were reported to be near.

Just before we completed our first orbit, I heard the engine decelerate slightly and noticed our rotor RPM had reduced a small amount, about 2 percent. All of this is normally controlled automatically by the governor on the engine (the same part that failed several years earlier), and there is a switch on the controls that allows us to manually adjust it. Every so often during a flight a very minor adjustment has to be made with this switch, so initially I wasn't concerned about it. I tried adjusting the RPM back up to 100 percent and noticed it was not responding in either direction. As a precaution, I came out of the turn heading north and quickly checked the engine instruments, which were normal. The helicopter can fly just fine with this issue, so thinking the switch had failed, I let Paul know what was up.

"Hey, man, I have an issue with the governor, I'm going to take us back," I told him as I began a gentle left turn back towards the airport.

Within a second or two of starting that turn, and with no further warning, the engine began losing power. Warning lights came on and the audible "engine out" warning tone began rapidly beeping at an incredibly loud level. Now, at this point I have to be completely honest. The first thought that came into my head was, "You have got to be sh*tting me. This can't be happening again!"

NOT THE BEST NEW YEAR'S EVE

I remember rapidly pushing up on that switch, thinking the governor had again failed and rolled the engine to idle. As we turned I began quickly looking outside for a place to land, and my heart sank. There were a few small streets within range, but they all had large trees, people, kids playing, and power lines. Nothing I was looking at was going to work and if we tried, there was a good chance we would kill citizens on the ground. We were in an older part of Las Vegas, and as I was quickly realizing, most of the power lines aren't buried there—they are above ground, and there are wires everywhere.

I then turned harder in the same direction and could hear Paul talking on the radio to our dispatcher. I was so loaded up at this point, the only thing I remember hearing him say was "444" and "roll medical." As we came out of the bank we had turned 180 degrees and were only a couple hundred feet off the ground. I looked at what remained for landing areas and saw two small streets, both with several power lines. I chose the better of the two, which turned out to be 23rd Street, just north of Bonanza.

As we descended towards 23rd Street I could tell we were going to be just short of it and actually impact a set of fifty-foot power lines that ran behind a house on a street called Margaret. I could see just past that set of large wires. If we were able to make it over the house they ran behind, there was another single wire crossing the street on 23rd. We would need to land just short of this single wire to avoid hitting it. A quick glance inside and I saw we were near the bottom limit of our rotor RPM. If this gets below a certain point, the blades will rapidly begin to slow—the helicopter will become uncontrollable and stop flying.

We have the ability to slow our rate of descent by using up rotor RPM, which essentially allows us to come down just a little bit slower. Although our RPM was already dangerously low, there was no other choice. I dragged it down just a little bit further as we cleared the wires and the house. I then aggressively pitched the nose up in a maneuver called the "flare," which is the last part of the autorotation maneuver. This slows the forward momentum and builds the rotor RPM, which helps cushion the landing at the very bottom as the helicopter is put back in a level attitude.

I remember the nose coming up, and as I began to pull up on the collective control to cushion the landing, the RPM quickly bled off. We were still at about twenty-five to thirty feet above the ground. I attempted to push forward and level us before we hit, but the helicopter stopped responding and the controls became very sluggish. In the next second we hit the street still in a somewhat nose-high attitude, the tail striking the ground first. The impact as we hit the ground was tremendous. For a split second there was an incredible pain in my lower back, then everything went black.

As I came to, the warning horn for the engine out was still blaring in my helmet and Paul was telling me to get out. I was in incredible pain. My back hurt so bad I could barely move. I began to realize the skids on the helicopter had collapsed and one of the rotor blades had detached, landing in the street about fifty yards away. Paul climbed out and came over to my side, struggling to get my door open. I told him I couldn't move and he unfastened my harness, slowly pulling me out of the ship. It was almost unbearable. He helped me over to the sidewalk and laid me down flat on my back, trying not to move me any more than necessary.

People began coming out of their houses and we could smell fuel leaking. We could also hear the engine igniters, powered by the electrical system, rapidly firing in an attempt to automatically restart the engine. Realizing there was a potential for a fire, Paul began yelling for the citizens to stay away. Although he was hurt, he then ran back up to the aircraft to pull the emergency fuel shut-off and kill the electrical system. After he came back over to my side, he stood in the street next to me and we could hear sirens approaching.

I remember slowly lifting my head up and looking towards the helicopter in the street. I was shocked to see that our tail section had completely separated and was in a driveway a few houses down. I looked over at Paul and said, "Dude, the ship is destroyed, I'm pretty sure my back is broken . . . how are you still walking around?!?!?!?"

NOT THE BEST NEW YEAR'S EVE

I think he was running on adrenaline at that point and it began to wear off. He pretty much sat on the ground with a groan as the first patrol officer arrived.

I vividly remember two things that happened as I was lying in the street. First, I was extremely cold and began shaking as I started to go into shock. Second, out of the several people to come out of their houses, not one person came over to help us. Some of them took their phones out to take pictures and record videos that would later end up on social media. One person posted a picture of me lying on the sidewalk that was later shared by a local media source. Even now it bothers me to remember it. My feeling has always been, regardless of what your opinion is of the police, at that moment there were two human beings lying in the street obviously hurt pretty bad. And yet not a single person tried to help. I have since tried to restore my faith in humanity by thinking maybe they were scared, overwhelmed, or just didn't know what to do. But it's an unfortunate reality that some people will always have a hatred towards police no matter how hard we try to bridge the gap.

It was at this point, after learning my lesson from the last time, that I pulled out my cell phone and called Ashley. Boom, right to voicemail. I called again and when she answered she sounded a little annoyed, telling me she was trying to get the girls down for a nap and could I call her back? That's when I barely got out, "Paul and I just crashed and I'm lying in the street." And then the call dropped. You can't make this stuff up.

As the first officer arrived, running over to us he looked pretty overwhelmed and wasn't sure how he could help. Our officers see and deal with all kinds of terrible situations, but this was certainly a first for him. He later rode with me in the ambulance to the trauma center and was the one that called Ashley to give her an update.

Arriving at the hospital was quite an experience. There was a large group of doctors and nurses waiting to receive us. I arrived first and could tell there were already a ton of officers and members of our department at the hospital. Many more would be arriving soon. Within seconds, my flight suit, along with everything else, was cut off and I vaguely remember them asking me lots of questions. There were a few minutes of what could be described as organized chaos before they rolled me to another room and put me in the CT scanner. It was at this point that fear really began to set in. All the hospital staff left the small room so the scan could be started and all of a sudden I was alone. I was still in the most pain I had ever experienced and my insides just didn't feel . . . right. Once the test was complete they brought me back into the trauma bay and that's when I saw Ashley.

Seeing her gave me comfort and a tremendous feeling of relief. I felt really bad for what she had to be going through but I knew that no matter what news they gave us we would deal with it together. She was somehow very composed and dealing with it remarkably well. As for me, not so much. As she has mentioned, I am not a fan of strong narcotic pain medicine. I don't like feeling out of it, and the medication has occasionally made me pretty nauseous in the past. So, like a complete idiot, I refused any pain meds. My thinking was, *I'm already in the most pain I have ever experienced in my entire life. If I end up getting sick right now, I don't think I could bear it.* I know, dumb. Paul, on the other hand, had a different opinion on this matter and pretty much sounded like he was having a great time in the bed next to me. Not that I'm ever looking to do this again, but note to self: next time, take the pain medicine.

After several hours at the hospital it was determined I had compression fractures in two vertebrae along my lower back and I had broken my left arm. Paul and I were discharged later that night. The slow process of healing was about to begin.

chapter nine

ELEPHANT CIRCLES

Ashley

A couple years ago Dave and I began sharing our story at law enforcement marriage conferences. Our hour-long session was organized into a PowerPoint full of pictures, video, and the infamous air traffic audio from the first non-crash. The only piece missing was my part on the power of community. Nothing I was writing felt like a powerful enough message. I typed, read, deleted, re-typed, and re-read, and the cycle continued for days. I knew what message I wanted to share but couldn't articulate it in a way that gave it justice. I prayed God would give me the wisdom to find the right words. I finally found those words when I attended a talk by Jen Hatmaker and she began to tell us a story about elephants.

When a female elephant is giving birth, all the other female elephants in her herd form a tight circle around her, face outwards, and stomp their feet wildly, acting as her personal bodyguards. They do this to send a clear sign to any predators that if they want to attack their sister while she is most vulnerable, they'll have to get through them first.

It struck me like the hand of God himself. That's it! That is the perfect analogy for our community. We all desire to be part of a community. I would imagine it stems from our primal days when we needed community to survive. That's not too far from the truth today. I hope you have a community, whether that be an online community, church community, neighborhood community, or, in my case, a police wives' community.

I'm fortunate to be part of a few amazing communities. Remember Auntie Nikki? Of course you do, you just read about her in the last chapter. We actually met at a baby gym class when our daughters were infants and became instant friends. (Now you understand why my daughters refer to her as their "auntie.") Through her I met the rest of our friends, who we affectionately refer to as our "Vegas family." Isn't it fantastic when you find friends who become family?

While I was at the hospital with Dave after the crash on New Year's Eve, Nikki took care of my two girls and her daughter, none of whom had napped. She also answered a million phone calls (by this time the news about what happened was all over the internet), and probably let our dogs in and out a million times to go to the bathroom. When she answered the phone that afternoon, she had no idea what was going on and without question, loaded her four-year-old into the car and drove to my house. I didn't have to ask because she knew what I needed. I pray everyone has one of those friends in their life because God knows we need them.

Asking for help is hard and I'm really bad at it. In the twenty-four hours after Dave crashed, I probably had hundreds of text messages checking on us and asking if we needed anything. "Thank you, we're good. I really appreciate it though!" was my standard reply. Straight up lies. I wasn't good. I had a two-year-old and a four-year-old, a husband in a back brace who couldn't get off the couch by himself, parents who had to fly back to Alaska leaving me with no help, and, to top it all off, I was two weeks out from breast reconstruction surgery. Why is it so hard to ask for help or even say yes when someone offers it? I'm not sure at what point this whole idea that I had to be super woman, super wife, and super mom got into my head, but I needed a reality check.

I'm part of an amazing police wives' group here in Vegas. We are really great at everything from rallying when something tragic happens to meal trains when a new baby is born. I'm really great at offering help, but this was the first time I'd been on the receiving end. My friend who heads up our wives' group knew better than to accept my "We're good" response. She set up a meal train, and for weeks fellow police families brought us dinner. That was such a relief. I don't know about you, but sometimes deciding what's for dinner can be one of the most stressful times of the day. Not having to think about it was such a weight off my shoulders. The outpouring of love and support was amazing. There were people we didn't know bringing our family dinner. This was a true testament to the power of community. We will forever be grateful for so many acts of kindness.

How do you explain to a two-year-old and a four-year-old why their daddy is in a back brace and can't pick them up? We told the girls daddy had an "owie back" and they needed to be careful around him until he was better. That explanation was good enough for them and at the time they didn't ask how he got hurt.

We had a lot of visitors in the weeks after the accident. It was probably a week after the accident when out of the blue our two-year-old asked Dave if he fell out of the helicopter. That's what she inferred from listening to conversations . . . Daddy fell out of the helicopter and hurt his back. To this day she is still wise beyond her years.

The first time that feeling of overwhelming anxiety came over me, I was standing in the kitchen doing dishes. I looked at our two little girls sitting at the table eating their snack and knew I needed help. My reconstructive surgery was two weeks away. I had contemplated pushing it back a few weeks (or months) but I needed to get the spacers taken out and the implants put in. I couldn't take a full breath because it hurt to fully expand my lungs. The spacers were hard as a rock and super uncomfortable. I would eventually need to go back to work. Dave's doctor's appointments and physical therapy filled up our calendar. We needed help. For the first time, I admitted I couldn't do it on my own. I needed my time in the middle of the elephant circle.

My sister lives in Seattle and works from home, so she was able to come and help. She and her four-month-old daughter came to stay with us for a few weeks. The reconstructive surgery would be nothing like the mastectomy, so I knew if I had just a little extra help I'd be able to make it all work.

The six months after Dave's accident weren't easy. There was a lot of juggling the girls, changing my schedule, taking time off work, and asking for help. But we got through it with the help of our family, friends, and police community. We can learn a lot from the elephants. There are so many people willing to stand around us and give us time to be vulnerable in the middle of the circle, if we let them.

Pride is what made it so uncomfortable for me to be in the middle of the circle. I've always thought of myself as a strong, independent woman who can get through anything. While that may be true, I struggle so much more when I try to do it all on my own. I have this fear that asking for help is putting someone out. Yet I'm always willing to help someone, and I never feel put out by doing so. Why is that? Why do we project our fears onto others and choose to not accept their help? I can't imagine that the female elephant worries about putting her sisters out when they are standing around her stomping their feet keeping her and her baby safe.

This season of my life really showed me the value of community. When I put my guard down and fully embraced my time in the middle of the circle, I learned the beauty in allowing people to help.

chapter ten

WHEN LIFE HANDS YOU LEMONS

Writing this book has brought up a lot of feelings, for both of us.

Ashley

They say when life hands you lemons, make lemonade. I'd say life has handed us some pretty interesting lemons over the past decade!

When you're living your story in real time it can feel overwhelming and never-ending. When you find yourself in that place, I'd like to encourage you to stop, take a breath, and shift your mindset. Instead of drowning in the "Why is this happening to me?" thoughts, ask yourself "how will this make me stronger?" I want to preface this by saying it isn't easy. It's taken me years to shift my mindset, and I still struggle with it. There have been so many times I've found myself questioning God and asking, "Why us? Haven't we been through enough?" Throughout some of the hardest seasons of our marriage there has always been this little voice inside saying, "Keep going."

Fear of the unknown almost got the best of me more times than I can count. So, what got me through? Faith and leaning into each other. I truly believe a life lived in fear creates obstacles, but a life lived in faith creates possibilities. Fear is an interesting word. Just reading it can induce physical responses. When you think of fear, does your heart race? Do you feel that lump rising in your throat?

It's really the unknown that we fear. We had a lot of unknowns, especially after the second engine failure. We didn't know what Dave's recovery time would be. We didn't know if he'd be able to fly again (physically or mentally). We didn't know how we'd manage with me working full time, two toddlers, another breast surgery, and Dave not being able to get off the couch by himself. There were so many times stress manifested itself into fear and anger, for both of us. We had to check ourselves and remember we are in this together. We couldn't let the stress of the situation pull us apart; we had to remain united.

You'll hear the word "compatibility" a lot when talking about marriage. There are online dating sites developed around this entire concept. How compatible are you and your partner? If Dave and I took one of those tests, I'm not sure we would've been marked as "compatible." Maybe we should take one and find out! That'll be in the next book. Being compatible is important, but it's really more about being united. The key to getting through any situation life throws your way is remaining united and committed to weathering the storm together. It's not always easy, but the best approach is to be proactive. Make the commitment to be on the same team before life gets tough. One of you (or both of you) may have to be reminded of the commitment you made every now and again because let's be honest, emotions get the best of us. We're only human.

After DVB's death, fear became a real obstacle in my life. There were many nights Dave would get called out on a rescue and I'd lie in bed tossing and turning with worry until that "I'm back" text came through. If it wasn't obvious, I don't show up as my best self when I'm sleep deprived. I had a choice to make. I could let fear get the best of me and worry myself sick (and exhausted) every time Dave went on a rescue, or I could ground myself in faith. Dave is exactly where he has been called to be. He is living out his true potential. He's an amazing pilot and loves what he does. I have faith in his abilities and even more faith in God's plan. If only we all had a crystal ball and could see the future—it'd make leaning into faith when fear creeps in easier, wouldn't it?

We've all heard the sayings "everything happens for a reason" and "life isn't fair." I used to agree with both those statements. Over the years I've changed my opinion; sometimes bad things just happen. There is no explanation for it. Sometimes life just isn't fair. When we feel the need to overanalyze every bad situation looking for the reason behind it, we slow down what really matters: progress and healing. Instead of racking your brain trying to figure out why, I'd challenge you to shift your mindset and focus on what can come from it. Could you and your partner lean into each other? Could you lean deeper into your faith? Could this situation find a way to propel you forward and not set you back? When DVB died, Dave questioned why. He couldn't understand why bad things happen to great people. He will never know the answer, and he's come to terms with that. Instead of dwelling on how he died, he chooses to celebrate how he lived.

The Pillars of Marriage

Marriage isn't 50/50. It's 100/100. It's each of us giving 100 percent effort and commitment to each other and our marriage. But let's be honest, there are times we can't both give 100 percent, and that's when the other half steps in to keep us whole. Marriage is a give and take in the sense that sometimes one person can only give 80 percent and the other person has to step up and give 120 percent. Here's the part to pay close attention to: the person stepping up has to do so without resentment. We all go through personal struggles. Just wait, your turn is coming.

It took us years to come to this realization. As we faced struggles in the beginning of our marriage, we both had unrealistic expectations that we both had to give 100 percent all of the time, no matter what, because our marriage depended on it. What our marriage really depends on is us working together as a team. We have to realize when someone is struggling and the other person has to step up and take the lead. Most of the time one of us is able to do that, but there have been low times when we both found ourselves struggling. What then? That's when perseverance and communication is crucial. We always talk about seasons, but in the especially hard times, we have to take it day by day, or hour by hour.

We all have tough seasons in life. Things are going to happen that we don't have control over. What we do have control over is how we deal with the situations as they arise. We can let life's storms push us apart, or we can fight for them to pull us together.

When life feels out of your control, anger is a pretty normal emotion. We've been angry. We've been angry with our situation, both in and out of our control, and we've allowed ourselves to become angry with each other. Hindsight is 20/20. (I'm killing it with the catchy sayings this chapter!) Reflecting on the past decade of our marriage, there were many times we should have been more united. We're on the same team. We both want the same outcome for our life and our family, sometimes we just have different ideas about how to get there. We've learned to fully embrace our differences and see the strength in them, which is why we affectionately refer to ourselves as "Team Callen."

Your marriage is the foundation of your family. It has to be built strong enough to weather the storms. If the foundation of your house gets damaged, you fix it before the house crumbles down on itself. The same goes with your marriage. You fix it before your life comes crumbling down around you.

Marriage isn't easy for anyone. It sure hasn't been easy for us. Our mission behind sharing our story and this book is to breathe hope into those who might be struggling. We have learned a lot of lessons along the way, some were harder to learn than others. We've laughed, cried, and done a lot of soul searching throughout this journey of putting our life into words people will actually be reading. Every emotion you felt reading this, we felt right along with you.

As this chapter, and book, comes to an end, I'd like to offer my own spin on the lemon saying:

When life hands you lemons, make lemonade, add some vodka, and throw a party.

www.ingramcontent.com/pod-product-compliance
Lightning Source LLC
LaVergne TN
LVHW041536060526
838200LV00037B/1015